Radical *Grace*

Radical *Grace*

Live Free *and* Unashamed

LAUREL APPEL

Appel Creations
PUBLISHING™
Holly Springs, NC

Published in the United States by Appel Creations
Holly Springs, NC 27540
USA

First printing, 2022

Book Cover Design by ebooklaunch.com
Book Interior Design by bbebooksthailand.com
Editing by David Ferris and Kimberly Stuart
Author Photograph by Zach Appel
Graphic Design by Zach Appel
Glyph Butterfly© Illustration by Laurel Appel

ISBN (eBook) 979-8-9855387-2-4
ISBN (HC) 979-8-9855387-1-7
ISBN (PB) 979-8-9855387-0-0

To my beloved, Phillip,
our cherished family,
and butterflies.

Table of Contents

We then, as workers together with Him also plead with you not to receive the grace of God in vain.

~ 2 Corinthians 6:1

For the law was given through Moses, but grace and truth came through Jesus Christ.

~ John 1:17

Stand fast therefore in the liberty by which Christ has made us free, and do not be entangled again with a yoke of bondage.

~ Galatians 5:1

Acknowledgments

I am eternally grateful for the inspiration and strength I received from God while on the journey of writing this book. Thank you, Jesus, for not only giving me your radical grace, freedom and healing, but for teaching me through your grace so I can share You with others.

Without the unfailing love, support, and encouragement of my best friend and husband, Phillip Appel, this book would never have existed. Phillip, there is so much of you in this book. Your commitment to both God's grace and to me, inspired me to find myself and eventually launched me into this project. Thank you for the endless discussions over coffee, for doing the dishes all those days I was glued to my keyboard, and for your honest and thoughtful input. Words cannot describe my gratitude and love.

Thank you, my wonderful and beloved children, Zach, Caitlyn, Michael, Taylor, and Calah, for your love and support not just for this project, but always. You will never know how much it means to me. You five are my favorite children and I love you all the most!

Thank you, my precious grand-princesses, Rain, Maddie, and Luna for bringing me joy and filling me up every moment I get to be with you. Your precious lives inspire me to encourage others to soak in the blessings of

God because that is what you are. Your LaLa loves you!

A special thank you goes to my sweet sister in Christ, Deanna Martin, who has been with me since day one of this journey. You have been my Barnabas for too many years to count. Thank you, my precious friend, for your love, encouragement, and support.

I must also thank Claudia Hawley, Charlene Cuomo, Adrienne Giordano, and Janelle Aby: my "firepit tribe." Your encouraging words and friendships are dearly treasured. I will forever sit by the firepit, share s'mores with you, and be here to root for you wherever God takes you. Thank you for cheering me on.

The Preface

I finally found me. The *real* me. Some might say God found me, but I would disagree. God has always known who and where I am. I have never been lost to Him. He made me and I'm pretty sure He has kept track of me all my life, no matter where I was. But He did show me the way to discover the authentic Laurel, the one who was lost because of her past. He helped me dig through the muck of despair that was clouding my vision of the real me. And that muck was keeping me from the life that He had created for me.

People who have only met me recently have no idea about the journey I have been on; how different I am compared to the younger me. See, I was sexually abused both as an infant and again as a preteen. The effects of that abuse on sweet little blond-haired Laurie were devastating. I was imprisoned by depression, anger, self-doubt, and negative self-talk. I felt unlovable, dirty, and shameful. I suffered from terrible anxiety which drove me to an obsessive-compulsive disorder in which I constantly counted my steps and repeated actions. I was prone to self-injury when I felt out of control. I ended up fearful of people and couldn't go out, even to the grocery store.

In the midst of this suffering, I was so thrilled to accept Jesus as a teenager. I started learning about His love for me and that my sins were paid for by Jesus on the cross. I wish I could tell you that just giving myself to Jesus fixed everything. It isn't true.

For years Phil, the kids, and I, would head off to church Sunday morning, Bibles in tow, to listen to the worship band and pastor's sermon, enjoy catching up with our friends, and heading to Casa Blanca afterwards with them for some New Mexican bacon wrapped green chile poppers and an hour or so of laughter. The food and fellowship were great, but once I got home, the cold reality set in; nothing I had heard that day in church made a difference in how I felt about myself. Nothing. I was still the same person I was when I left the house that morning, only with a belly aching a little from the poppers.

The gospel I had heard didn't free me like I thought it would. Though, I knew that I had eternal salvation, I was still a wreck. And for a long time, I thought that was just the way it was going to have to be. So, I accepted it. I accepted the gospel of "trying to clean myself up" which was the idea that I could become more righteous and holy merely by doing good works and avoiding sin.

While I now recognize it is erroneous (and destructive), this concept made sense to me at the time. I could make myself right and good by working at it. It was like compulsively counting steps. It sounded like a good plan to me. It was a way of taking matters into my own hands. And I did.

But it didn't produce the change I sought. My marriage, children, and life were suffering, and I desperately needed answers. I needed to find myself, the real me, not the one I was pretending to be. So, I started praying specifically for that. How could I unbury myself from the muck of despair I had been trapped in for so long? I had to start walking toward God, and that was the beginning of my journey.

Eventually, I realized the one thing that cut right through that muck: His grace. But it's not just the grace we learn about at church. You know the verse, the one about us being saved by grace, which is amazing, for sure. I got that, and that secured my eternity. That grace reveals the abundance of God's love for us that He would die for our sins so we could spend eternity with Him. Some define it as **G**od's **R**iches **A**t **C**hrist's Expense.

I'm talking about another kind of grace that washes away the grime of shame that gets caked on us from this world, from day-to-day monotony and working hard to be holy to the extreme of depression and suicidal thoughts. I'm talking about a revolutionary and extreme kind of grace. A type of grace that awakens us out of the deadness of this world and makes us alive and free. This sort of grace is one that very few people talk about. I'm talking about radical grace.

I can testify that when I truly got God's radical grace, my life started to change. I remember the moment when it first hit me. I was lying on our burgundy leather couch (southwest style is all the rage in New Mexico!), reading through Galatians chapters 3, 4, and 5 repeatedly. For some reason, I just knew they held some secret that was going to help me to unlock the real, authentic me. I prayed for the Spirit to help me see what I couldn't see. I was like the persistent widow in the Book of Luke. I kept reading it and asking God for insight, and I didn't stop until I got an answer.

Suddenly a light bulb came on, and I finally got what Paul was telling me in those passages. GRACE! Radical grace! I *thought* I had understood grace, but I realized at that moment that grace changed much more of my life than I had been taught. God's radical grace is not only for our salvation, but it governs our daily lives and inspires us to live now; *really* live and walk by faith. It is transformational when applied to our relationships, including with God, as well as the proper perspective of our sinful nature. I wish I could define it for you in one succinct sentence, but I can't because it involves understanding a host of topics such as the law, sin, the covenants, our dual natures in Christ, the Holy Spirit, and the commandments of Jesus. That is why I wrote this book. Getting the full version of radical grace won't happen by reading a one-liner on a tee shirt or a coffee mug. It is going to take a little time, some storytelling, and a little digging into the Bible.

After that, I couldn't unsee it. I knew that radical grace was missing from my life.

That day, God had started me down the path of healing and discovery. It took several more years to untie all the knots that a graceless life had tied me up in, but now that I am walking unbound and living a life of peace, joy, and love, I am excited to share what I have discovered with you.

That life is what I want for you, my friend. You have picked up this book simply because of curiosity or because you are searching for something more, different. Whatever the reason, you chose to spend your time with me within the pages of this book and I want this time together to be a blessing to you. I imagine we are sitting in my living room, enjoying a snack and a cup of coffee or tea, and conversing about grace. As we lean into Jesus and His amazing radical grace together, I will be vulnerable and share myself with you in hopes that you will open yourself up to God, be vulnerable to Him, as He pours Himself and His love into your soul. I pray through our time together that you truly understand and fully receive God's healing, amazing, wonderful radical grace.

Laurel
Holly Springs, NC, December 2022

CHAPTER 1

The Reason

Why radical grace?

Red juice splattered the room where I stood, frustrated, next to my infant son in his crib as he cried, profusely. I had just hit the wall, physically when I hurled his bottle at it, but also emotionally and mentally.

I was 24 years old, depressed, stressed, and at the peak of my agoraphobia (fear of public places). My marriage was hanging on by a thread, my husband, Phil, was a full-time engineering student at college by day and worked full-time at a hospital during the graveyard shift, and there I was, in the middle of the night, with a baby boy that wouldn't sleep and wouldn't stop crying. I had spent the last twenty years keeping it together, hiding my shame, excelling in everything so I could cover up how awful I felt about myself. That dreadful night was when it all reached my breaking point.

I was an exhausted new mom without the faintest idea of how to care for another human being. I had gone into my son's room several times to see if I could convince him to go to sleep to no avail. I picked up his bottle of juice…okay, so you seasoned moms are thinking, why juice? No wonder he wasn't sleeping. Yeah, I could have used your sage advice back then.

Anyway, I took that bottle and pitched it at the wall as if I was Orel Hershiser on the mound at Dodger Stadium. My voice cracked as I screamed in despair. The bottle broke and juice went flying everywhere. Red dots spotted the walls like it had the chicken pox, and tears poured down my face as I realized that I couldn't do this anymore. I was at the end of my rope.

As I fell to the floor, broken and sobbing, crippling thoughts filled my mind. *I don't want to be this kind of mommy. Am I capable of abusing my child? Am I going to allow the effects of my childhood abuse to be inherited by my own children? I am tired of trying. I can't do it anymore.*

These thoughts scared me to my core. I knew something had to change. I also knew that I couldn't fix myself on my own. If God would speak to me, I would listen.

We all have our unique story. You may have a pivotal point in yours, like this juice fit I had, that woke you up to the knowledge that something had to drastically change. Maybe it was a devastating medical diagnosis, the death of a loved one, or hitting rock bottom somehow. Maybe that pivot point is taking place right now as you find yourself feeling lifeless or thirsting for an elusive freedom that you thought you would obtain by receiving Christ, yet it remains out of reach.

I found that freedom, and I want to share it with you. It took time, but I did finally discover the pure and revolutionary grace of God that extended that freedom to me and healed my soul.

I am free from that old self, free from trying to do the impossible of making myself right, and free from thinking I am unworthy of anything good. I am free in God's radical grace, and you can be too.

I want you to understand something vital. Knowing grace to the extent that I have discovered hasn't made everything in my life perfect. There are two factors that still affect me: the world, which includes the devil, and my flesh that is influenced by it. I make mistakes. I'm guilty sometimes. I still have bad days, get angry, deal with physical and emotional pain. The difference, though, between me now and me thirty years ago is that I recognize that those reactions are the old me and I don't need to beat myself up over my mistakes. I know that while I still have my flesh hanging around, more importantly, I have been made new, holy, and righteous by Jesus' blood. I'm born again. I'm forgiven, clean, and whole. That is the new me and my true identity.

So, I have become authentically Laurel. I accept who I am. I desire to live a life of love, forgiveness, and grace, but I also accept the fact that I mess up sometimes. I'm just going to be the best me, by the Spirit of God, and when my flesh gets out of control and messes up, I apologize, do what I can to rectify the damage, and I move on. I don't mean to sound flippant; I am in no way minimizing my sin. I understand the magnitude of my actions and how they affect others. Simply, I am saying that I understand I have a flesh. Like Paul the apostle writes about in the Book of Romans, sometimes I do not do what I want to do. It is not me that does it, but the sin in me. I have come to accept my existence, for now, as a two-part person, consisting of my flesh and my spirit. Thankfully, because I understand God's radical grace, I land in the love camp more often and more quickly than I used to. I also have a peace and joy that are an unmovable foundation in my life.

And to be honest, I look at others authentically too, recognizing they too have two natures if they are in Christ. I realize you have a flesh, you make mistakes, but at the same time you are a child of God and are renewed in your mind and spirit. I accept you; warts, mistakes, and all. I also see the beauty of who you are in your spirit because that is *your* new identity. This has been a big revelation for me. And it might be for you too.

Through this process of learning about God's radical grace, Phil and I have learned that most people suffer from some form of self-doubt. I'm sure we all expect that from people who have had trauma or have struggled with unrighteousness, whether it be self-inflicted or inflicted by others. But we are not alone. People raised in a great family by parents who love them and even have grown up in the church also deal with the consequences of living in a world that reminds them they are not perfect.

The typical answer to this issue in our Christian culture is to work on our sin, try to become a better person, and do good things to help counter the bad stuff. However, through our years in ministry, we have found that answer isn't really solving anyone's problems.

I will share a story with you as an example of what I am talking about. There was always a huge turn-out when one of the local churches would bring in an evangelist to the little town in New Mexico in which we lived and ministered. Many people in the community would gather at the convention center to hear their message.

Each year something struck Phil and I as odd. At the end of the speech the speaker would offer an altar call. They would ask people to come forward if they wanted to receive Jesus as their Savior. It was a beautiful thing to watch people make a public dedication to Jesus. However, the odd thing was that people would go forward who had already given their lives to the Lord and had been attending church for years.

Why would these believers feel the need to accept their Savior *again*? Perhaps they didn't feel like they were saved, and they wanted to make sure they were. But why would they doubt their salvation? Because they still sinned, and they had been told that their sin was separating them from God and was an indicator that they weren't doing enough to be righteous or holy. They weren't living up to the expected moral standard. I know those feelings. I lived with them for many years.

It is a common experience, and it is time to stop this terrible cycle that is pushing people either into a life of shame and doubt or pushing them away from the church entirely. This tragic situation is caused by the widespread misinterpretation of the gospel by our faith leaders. This book represents a break from that. My intent is to redefine grace as radical and to free you into your new life.

What about that abundant life Jesus promised? What if you could have a life that is rich with love, full of the Spirit of God, and marked by joy and peace? What if you could be authentically you? What if you could let go of all the anger, negative self-talk, and doubt that plagues you? What if God really did put all your pieces back together, heal you of your past, and show you that you have a blessed future? What if you felt free? What if you truly felt alive again?

He can do this. He did it for me. His grace is radical, and that is what has inspired me to write this book.

What is so different about the Gospel message presented in this book than the one you can hear any Sunday morning?

This book is based both on pure Biblical theology and my story. Every scripture that I mention, or paraphrase, is listed by chapter in the back of this book. Take some time to review them. My desire is for you to see my transformation as we explore the Biblical concepts that facilitated that transformation. Radical grace is the thread that ties everything together.

We will travel back to the early days when Jesus and the writers of the New Testament were teaching people about the good news of Jesus' coming. And as we explore each building block of the Gospel, you will see Christ's revolutionary love for you, what He has done so He could spend forever with you, and we will rediscover the lost and forgotten promises of God's Word. We will carefully step through each topic based in scripture and I will give some practical examples so you can understand and apply what I present to you.

I would imagine that most protestant theologians agree that it is by grace and grace alone that we are saved. I believe the Bible teaches that grace is not only for our ultimate salvation and trip into eternity, but also for today. God's grace is given to us every day and we are to share that same grace with others. Grabbing ahold of grace to the extreme changed me and can change you too.

This book has some answers you might be looking for, but it's not a "how-to" book, it's a "who-to" book. Let's take a fresh look at Jesus and His mission and unlock your freedom as we thoroughly explore God's radical grace.

In preparation for our adventure together, though, I would ask you to leave your baggage behind; especially the baggage of burdensome or mistaken Biblical teachings that weighs you down. Approach this book with an open mind. I will teach you a concept of grace that probably challenges many of your long-held conventions. That is the nature of being "radical."

Go ahead, grab a snack and a cup of coffee, and let's get going on this life-changing journey to discovering God's radical grace.

CHAPTER 2

The Change

It's not about sin, it's about grace.

I *am worthless. God can't love me because I'm not good enough. I should be a better Christian. I am so broken that if I don't get better, I'm going to lose my husband. He will want to leave me for someone who isn't so messed up. Maybe he is already looking. Don't make a mistake or show anyone that you are as pathetic as you are. I need to be a better person. I wish I could be normal. I don't care if I live or not. How can anyone love me?*

Such was the nagging, miserable pattern of my constant negative self-talk. These days it is much better. Here is me now:

My hair! It looks terrible. This shirt makes me look fat, well...that's because I am fat. I should lose weight. Or buy bigger shirts. That lady was so rude to me. She doesn't like me for some reason. What did I say? Did I do something that made her not like me? I hope our new neighbors don't decide I'm too weird. Well, you are weird, Laurel. They will see it. But will that make them run? They probably will, but I hope not.

My negative self-talk remains, but it is no longer so disparaging, depressing, and debilitating. And my thoughts are getting less and less negative as the years go on. I might be on the verge of buying bigger shirts.

How about you? What are you saying to yourself?

It is bad enough people say mean things to others, but we are often our own worst critic! Why do we judge ourselves so harshly? Why don't we accept ourselves? Why can't we like ourselves, let alone love ourselves?

Sadly, negative self-talk plagues everyone to some degree. A National Science Foundation study found that the average person has about 12,000 to 60,000 thoughts per day, of which a staggering 80% are negative!"[1]

Why do we beat ourselves up so severely? I believe it is because we are not confident in our value and standing with God. It's bad enough we are pressured by society to be beautiful, fit, rich, smart, and have a great sense of humor. All of these can lead to negative thoughts about ourselves as we don't measure up. However, we are also pressured within the Christian body to perform well, obey God, and stop sinning so much or so often. The outside pressure exacerbates our own inward feelings of failure and self-doubt. Many of us feel like we can never be good enough.

I would say stay off Instagram and go hide in a cave in the middle of a jungle somewhere, but even then, we would beat ourselves up because we weren't doing enough for God, and we'd etch our failures into the cave walls so we could "reflect" on them later. Then we would spend our days staring at those walls feeling defeated, dismal, and depressed. So, how do we stop that destructive voice?

There is an answer. It is the "who-to" I referred to previously. I'll explain.

I would guess that negative self-talk isn't an invention of modern times. Think about Zacchaeus, the woman caught in adultery, and the Samaritan woman at the well. I can only imagine that all three of them were also plagued by self-criticism. After all, they were the sinners of their time and society made sure they knew it. They most likely felt guilty, dirty, and unlovable.

As you recall, Zacchaeus was a short tax collector who climbed a tree so he could see Jesus walking down the street. Tax collectors were viewed as despicable sinners, and because of that, I would guess that the words *"you are an awful sinner,"* bounced around in his head quite a bit.

Jesus invited Himself to have dinner at Zacchaeus' house. While others called Zacchaeus a sinner, Jesus called him a son of Abraham. Zacchaeus was saved that day and forever changed because of his faith. Jesus is the great transformer.

It wasn't about Zacchaeus' sin; it was about Jesus loving him. It was about grace.

Another example: Jesus was teaching in the temple when some religious leaders brought to Him a woman who had been caught in adultery. Those men dragged her before the Lord to be stoned as the law required. They were testing Him, while judging and condemning her. I can only imagine the negative self-talk she lived with every day of her life. But did Jesus condemn her? No, and after He wrote something in the dirt that must have convinced her accusers that they weren't qualified to pick up a stone and judge her, she watched as they all walked away. Instead of condemning the woman, Jesus showed her His love for her, and she learned about grace that day.

It wasn't about her sin; it was about Jesus loving her. It was about grace.

Finally, we learn that the Samaritan woman at the well had been the wife of several husbands. The Jewish people were raised not to interact with or even speak to the people of Samaria, who were regarded as inferior. Her negative self-talk was probably a daily grind. But she was curious about this Jewish man at the well who ignored the social mores and spoke to her kindly. She ended up receiving Jesus as her Savior. This woman was forever changed by her encounter with Jesus.

It wasn't about her sin; it was about Jesus loving her. It was about grace.

All three of these people were called sinners, judged by those around them, and I'm sure felt unworthy of Jesus' love and forgiveness because they knew they were not perfect. But Jesus didn't come to condemn them because they were imperfect sinners, He came to save them because they were valuable to Him. He changed their lives and their eternal destination. He came to offer His love and radical grace.

For me to become nicer to myself, I had to take the long way around, through a poor imitation of grace first, before I became more forgiving and loving of myself.

Because of the childhood sexual abuse I endured, I felt guilty, dirty, and unworthy of love. When I started going to church, I went looking for freedom and something new, but sadly, I left feeling like I hadn't done enough, I sin too much, and I need to be more holy. The gospel I had heard was one that condemned me instead of freeing me. It constantly reminded me that because of my sin, I was guilty, dirty, and God was going to be disappointed in me unless I cleaned myself up. And that message amplified my feeling that I was unlovable because it made my sin the focus. This message *fueled* my negative thoughts rather than healed them. The gospel I kept hearing failed to transform me like I had expected it to.

Why didn't that false gospel have the power to change me? Because the emphasis was always my sin rather than God's grace. The true and complete gospel is all about grace and freedom in Christ. I had to learn about His grace to be transformed and released from the bondage of such negative thoughts, self-condemnation, and shame. See, the gospel is frequently muddled up with useless rules, misinformation, and confusion about our spiritual state in Jesus. God's grace is often overshadowed by the preoccupation of obedience and the work of trying to sin less as you do more. That lack of grace is what produces guilt, shame, and negative self-talk in our minds. It had that effect on me until I refused to let it anymore.

After years of trying to curb my anger, judgement, and shame about my past and how that was affecting my marriage, I realized that living well and healing my scars wasn't a matter of me fixing my sin by my own efforts, it was about Jesus and what He has already done for me.

See, I am Zacchaeus, the woman caught in adultery, and the woman at the well. Have I committed their specific sins? Maybe, maybe not. That doesn't matter anyway. Like them, it was my shame that was standing between me and Jesus. But with each of us, He cuts right through that wall of shame with His grace and gives us a new identity. That was what transformed our Biblical friends, and that's what transformed me.

Grace is what allows forgiveness and heals deep wounds. It isn't about trying to become righteous and quell shame through certain acts and behaviors; it is about His righteousness that He has graciously bestowed upon me. It isn't about me at all; it is about Jesus.

Before I came to understand radical grace, I lived through many struggles and much suffering. Sometimes I felt like I was dead, like there was no life in me, no inspiration or hope. Thoughts of suicide entered my mind. I understand and now live in the grace God offers. I found His boundless freedom within that grace that has broken the chains not only of my sin but also the chains my offenders had put me in. I am free! The answer is

Jesus and His radical grace! He changes us.

Figuring this all out was a journey that took several years. Through prayer, correct teaching, digging into the Word for myself, and getting to know the "who-to," Jesus, and His radical grace, I went from a fearful, guilty wreck to a faithful and freed child of God. I was transformed.

My friend, I want that same freedom for you! I want you to know God loves you and will never leave you. I want you to live in the peace and joy that freedom through His grace gives you. I want you to stop telling yourself what a failure you are. I want you to quit making sin and the effort to avoid it your focus in life. I want you to stop writing your failures on your cave walls. I want you to live free, enjoy life, and love much. I want you to truly understand and grab hold of God's grace and never let go. You should feel alive! Let Jesus' radical grace break your chains and be the change you need.

CHAPTER 3

The Bible

It's all about Jesus.

A talking donkey.
Giants.
The sun standing still.
A child named Maher-Shalal-Hash-Baz.
A woman turned into a pillar of salt.

Those are just a sliver of the strange and wondrous things recorded within the Bible's pages. They certainly add interest to God's Word, but all those fascinating details are not why the Bible is translated into 683 languages, sells over 100 million copies annually, and is in fact the most stolen book in the world.[2]

The reason the Bible is so sought after is, whether people realize it or not, because of its message of *radical grace*. However, despite the enduring relevance of the Bible, why are more than 50% of Americans not reading it?[3] I'd like to share a couple experiences that I think reveal the answer.

At a church my beloved Phil and I had recently started attending, they were promoting a book that was a substitute for the Bible. The pastor was excited to present it to the congregation. He encouraged us to place our "old" Bibles on the shelf and pick up this new version because it contained "most" of the Bible, and it was "easier to read."

However, it was selective in which books and which parts of each book it included. Phil and I did the math on it and found that over 80% of the text of the Bible had been cut from this condensed version. This one act of replacing the Bible with a new "easier to read" version not only disgraced God's Word but also discouraged people from reading their Bible because, they were told, reading the complete version was supposedly too much of a chore. But if people are discouraged from reading the entire Bible, in all its wisdom and glory, how can they fully know God and His radical grace?

The pastor read from this new version the part where God gave Moses the law from atop Mt. Sinai. He told us that it was our job to try to fulfill the law now that we are Christians.

Phil and I just looked at each other in surprise. Like many Christians, this pastor believes that it is believers' job to obey the Jewish law, which most people think of as the Ten Commandments. However, Christians' obedience to the other six hundred, or so, Jewish laws is not often clearly defined. He didn't mention them either.

Though, there are others, Phil and I included, who believe the Bible definitively states that Jesus fulfilled the requirements of the Old Covenant law, thus freeing His followers from that duty. The Bible teaches that trying to fulfill the law perfectly is impossible and that is why

Jesus came to fulfill it, forgive us for our inability to do so, and give us what we need to walk in righteousness. This understanding emphasizes faith in the righteousness of Jesus by His grace rather than working for righteousness, acceptance, approval, or rewards through obedience to the Jewish law. This is what the apostle Paul defined as grace versus works.

Sadly, many churches we have attended in recent years have taught that we are to be obedient, work on our sin, and strive to become more like Jesus. Where is grace? Why is grace being left out when it is *the* thing we should be talking about?

No wonder people aren't reading their Bibles. They are being told they might not be able to understand it if they tried to read it and that it is a big book of rules they need to stop breaking. Where is the hope of freedom in that?

I know that these pastors are only teaching what they themselves have been taught. Our Christian culture often promotes this principle of working on our own holiness through obedience rather than resting in the blessings of our new life in Christ. Isn't it time we end the cycle of legalistic condemning teaching that places such huge burdens on people to be sinless and that give rise to crippling shame and self-doubt? Who wants to read a book that is presented as a message from a God that is disappointed in you because you fail at His to-do list? You end up feeling ashamed because you just can't seem to achieve a moral standard that you should *obviously* be able to achieve. And when the focus is on the works of your flesh, you aren't talking about what you *can* do in your new spirit that you received by faith through God's grace.

Don't let anyone tell you that your life is defined by your sin and the effort to prevent it or discourage you from seeking out the truth about God's grace. When you avoid what He says by not reading the Bible, you are not only avoiding Him, but you are denying yourself the beautiful experience of seeing His grace woven through-out the pages of His Word. Once you understand that God's grace is real and radical, your eyes will be opened to the truth of the Word, and it will come alive to you. It has for me.

Usually, when we take time in the Word, our focus is on a particular topic, verse, or passage. Since the Bible has over 31,000 verses, our study of it can last a lifetime, and we still might not grasp all it contains. This is a great goal, but it is just as valuable to rise above all the detailed study and look at the big picture. Looking at the big picture helps us to see more clearly God's character, who we are to Him, and His gracious plan He had all along for humanity. Keeping the big picture in mind when we interpret the meaning of scripture helps us to avoid being led away from the truth.

I see three "big picture" concepts in the Bible. Let's review them briefly because they are the backbone on which we will be building our renewed understanding of God's grace. These are quick overviews of these concepts in which we will dig into more thoroughly throughout the rest of this book.

The first big picture concept is that everyone is born into sin and is therefore unrighteous, and we cannot make ourselves righteous through our own effort. The Bible begins with God creating the world. Then in Genesis chapter three we read the story of Adam and Eve, who disobeyed God's command not to eat from the Tree of the Knowledge of Good and Evil. Sin entered the world, and consequently, all humans are now *born* into sin, including you and me.

The sinful nature of humanity is evident throughout the Old Testament as we read about the failures of both the Gentiles and the people of God. Like the great King David, a *man after God's own heart*, our flesh gets the best of us. And with sin came death. The Jewish law was given so we would become aware we are not righteous. Through reading the Old Testament, we realize we need God's grace. Obeying the law couldn't make us righteous, and to be with God we must be righteous.

We need God's radical grace.

The second big picture concept is that God had a plan for the predicament we find ourselves in. Notice how quickly we come to the promise of a remedy for the "fall of man." You can find the first hint of this plan in Genesis 3:15 when God cursed the serpent for his role in

Adam and Eve's disobedience saying, "He shall bruise your head, and you shall bruise His heel." Then, by chapter 12 of Genesis, God promised Abram He would make an everlasting covenant with him and his descendants, in which, He promised all the nations would be blessed. This is the Abrahamic Covenant; the New Covenant that Jesus spoke about during Passover before His death. This deal that God made with Abraham was all about grace.

God's radical grace has been the plan all along.

The third big picture concept is the fulfillment of the promise to Abraham: Jesus, who is the solution to our sin and death problem and the answer for our new life. Jesus' life, death, resurrection, and ministry are the good news of the Gospel of Grace. Jesus' ministry was to conquer sin and death and impart His righteousness on those who have faith in Him and His righteousness. His mission is not our mission. His mission has been accomplished. "It is finished," as He so famously said (John 19:30). In Christ, we have a very different mission than working to "conquer our sin," "be a better person," or "try to sin less." We will be delving into that more throughout this book!

Jesus *is* radical grace.

The big picture of the Bible reveals the mess we find

ourselves in, but it also shows us there is a solution to fix that mess. When I first became a believer, I was filled with erroneous information about what really mattered. This experience is unfortunately common to many. When I accepted the Lord, I knew that upon putting my faith in Him, Jesus would save me from my sins, and I would receive eternal life. Yet, it wasn't until years later that I was taught one little thing that sparked a flame in me so bright and hot that it changed me immensely and drove my journey to eventually discovering radical grace. What did I learn? "It is all about Jesus." The entire Bible is about Jesus.

In fact, it was Phillip who taught me that. He had been a Christian all his life and when he was called to be a pastor, this was one of his phrases he used all the time. The first time I heard it I thought, *"The Bible is all about Jesus? Really? Even the Old Testament?"*

It *is* all about Him, from Genesis to Revelation. He is the foundation upon which everything else is built. He is the purpose and reason for the design. He is the root of the interpretation of the passages and author of the Bible. It's all about Jesus. And if it's all about Jesus, it's all about grace.

Luke tells a story of Cleopas and another man, who while walking to Emmaus, were talking about the death of Jesus of Nazareth. Jesus, now resurrected and apparently unrecognizable, came up and walked beside them and began speaking to them. Jesus told them about the plan God had for a Savior to come and He showed them evidence of this Savior in the scriptures, starting with

Genesis and ending with the books by the prophets. He most likely referenced what God had said to the serpent and His promise to Abram in the Book of Genesis!

Once the travelers arrived at their destination, they invited this mystery man in to have a meal. When Jesus broke the bread, their eyes were opened to who this stranger truly was. I love the men's response. They said that their hearts had burned within them while Jesus spoke and opened the scriptures to them.

Why did their hearts burn within them? I believe it is because they realized Jesus is the Messiah, or Savior. They were moved by seeing Him revealed to them within the scriptures. It made Him real. He was the Savior they had been waiting for. In that moment, they understood there was a plan since the beginning of humanity that was fulfilled by Jesus' death and resurrection. They were witnessing that plan as it unfolded before their very eyes. It made them realize God is bigger than, say, a Sabbath worship session in the synagogue. They realized God's grace was radical.

I understand their reaction! Once I realized the entire Bible is about Jesus, my response to the Word became a burning in my heart. I started by believing what Jesus said was true; that He was able to speak about Himself starting at Genesis and throughout the entire Old Testament. I was amazed by that fact and wanted to see it for myself. I started looking for Jesus and I realized we can find Him foreshadowed and prophesied about all throughout the Old Testament scriptures.

In doing that exercise, I realized Jesus was the fulfillment of God's plan of radical grace. If we leave Jesus out of any part of the Bible, we remove grace, and if we remove grace, we eliminate the reason for and purpose of Jesus. The Bible exists to teach us about God's grace through Jesus.

Not only are there foreshadows and prophesies about Jesus, but every word in the Bible points to Jesus in some way. In the Old Testament, sometimes the story is an allegory of Jesus and salvation, like the story of Noah and the flood, while other times the Bible describes our pitiful situation without Jesus and why we need God's grace. One such example is the Book of Judges. The Nation of Israel struggled with the influence of the pagan communities surrounding them. Through that book we see humanity was in dire need of a Savior, but even in those struggles, we see God's grace as He stepped in and touched the lives of the people we read about.

The same is true for you. When you read these stories, and view them considering God's grace, you will be amazed at how the scriptures come to life. My desire is for your heart to burn within you as you spend time with the Word. Never forget, the Bible is all about Jesus. No matter what book, chapter, or verse you are reading, you can find Him and His purpose in it if you always filter what you read through the big picture of Jesus and His radical grace. And when you do that, difficult to understand passages will become much easier to comprehend and seemingly contradictory verses will suddenly make sense.

Pastors seem conflicted in how they encourage their

flock to read the Bible. On the one hand, they emphasize its importance, but on the other hand, they seem to avoid urging people to read the full versions and those that are regarded as closest to the original text. This can lead to stripped-down substitutions like the sort I mentioned before.

The Bible is a love letter from your Creator God to you personally. He has things to show you and share with you. There is action, adventure, humor, romance, and suspense within its pages. There are quantum physics and miracles that defy our understanding of this world. Many enthralling family stories are included. Stories that tell of hard times and triumphs, revenge and redemption, and murder and new birth. A chronicle of a man who is God, who came and changed everything when He was born. He came for you personally. He died and rose again so He could be with you forever. He loves you.

The Bible is full of precious treasure! Let's engage in its complete richness and fullness.

The Bible, in its entirety, demonstrates Jesus' love for you and His plan to save you from the consequences of Adam's disobedience into which you have been born. This plan of grace was put in place because He wants to spend now and forever with you. It shows you your purpose in this life and for eternity. It shows you that you were created to be loved by Him, worship and love Him back, and love others. It demonstrates how it is Jesus' mission to make you righteous so you can be with Him both now and after you walk through the door to eternity.

I pray you will see Jesus' love for you and know that His only desire has ever been to make sure you and He could hang out forever because He really digs you. And this book He put together reveals the means to do just that. He made it possible by His radical grace.

CHAPTER 4

The Fall

By grace we are saved.

"Help! Help! Dad! Anyone! Help!" I was screaming at the top of my lungs for someone to come save me as I was hanging on for dear life.

I was only six years old.

My dad was a Jeep nut. During my young childhood years, he would take our family on many adventures with our Jeep club. That day, we had spent several hours bouncing around inside my dad's 1970 Jeep CJ touring the town of Tin Cup, Colorado. All the Jeeps and their people had stopped for lunch near a creek in the woods. Dad gathered wood to start a campfire and Mom prepped the hotdogs for roasting and unpacked all the fixings, including the pork and beans. The Little Debbie snacks and orange sodas were set out as well.

Meanwhile, my older brother, David, and I were glad to get out of the Jeep, stretch our legs, and start exploring. He is two years older than me and had more experience, so I deemed him my leader and followed him. I knew he would have some grand adventure for us.

Off we went. To the creek, of course.

We travelled along the side of the creek looking for a good place to cross because, well, that's what you do when you are an explorer faced with a creek with no manmade bridge. We came to a spot where several large boulders rested in the creek bed, providing a series of steppingstones to reach the other side. This was it. This was the place we were going to forge forth into the unknown.

My brother and his long legs hopped from the first boulder, to the next, and then the next until he arrived on the bank of the creek opposite me and was off discovering what he could find in the woods.

I followed. I hopped from the first boulder to the next... well, not exactly. My short legs and I didn't make it and I fell between the first two huge rocks. My instinct was to grab ahold of something, and I dug my fingernails into a slight ridge in the side of the slick, well-worn river rock facing me. The ridge wasn't much thicker than my nails.

My torso and legs flung out down river, and as I hung sideways in the rushing water between the two boulders, adrenaline and the cold water had me shaking. Terror struck as I was sure I was going to wash away any second. My shoes came off my heels and for some stupid reason I was focused on trying not to lose them, or my pants. My jeans got heavy once they were saturated. I imagined they would find me downstream dead and naked. Dead wasn't good. But naked too? How embarrassing!

Digging my fingernails into the ridge on the rock in front of me, I tensed up and held on for my life. If I tried to move at all, or tried to pull myself up, my fingernails would start to slip off the rock. I was helpless. I started screaming.

At that moment, I knew I needed someone to save me.

To appreciate the magnitude and beauty of what Jesus did for the world, we need to grasp the predicament we were in without Him.

I can't imagine too many people, believers and unbelievers alike, don't already understand that the Christian faith is about knowing we need a Savior. So why am I dedicating a whole chapter to such an elementary concept? Because you might need to be reminded about your unrighteousness. Being born into sin means you cannot claim your innocence; you are considered guilty from birth. I'm not telling you this to shame you, but rather to free you.

We read in the Book of Genesis about the "fall of man." Adam and Eve, the first man and woman created, lived in the garden of Eden. God told them not to eat from the Tree of the Knowledge of Good and Evil. However, Eve was tempted and deceived by the serpent, and she ate the fruit from the tree.

I must take a moment and say that I don't believe that

fruit was an apple. Apples have gotten a bad rap because at some point someone decided it was the fruit from the garden. Maybe I'm biased because of my last name. I don't know.

Anyway, she then offered the *not apple* to Adam, and he ate it as well. Because they are the parents of all of humanity, this act of disobedience has impacted all of humankind in that from that day forth all people born on this planet are born into unrighteousness. That unrighteous nature hangs around until we shed it on our way through the door into *forever* with Jesus.

As if unrighteousness wasn't bad enough, Paul the apostle tells us because sin came into the world, death came in also.

In addition to this bad news, Paul tells us that we cannot live in eternity if we are unrighteous. He tells us flesh and blood can't inherit the kingdom of God and corruption can't inherit incorruption. Just like oil and water don't mix, sin and righteousness don't mix either.

And it is at this moment, we realize, we need someone to save us.

Have you ever thought about the fact that folks like Billy Graham and Mother Teresa were born into unrighteousness? For all the good and righteous things they did while alive, they still had a sinful flesh. They needed a Savior just like you and me. Their one-way ticket to heaven didn't depend on how much good either of them did in their lives, nor did it depend on how much bad they avoided or committed. Like them, your salvation has nothing to do with what you do, good or bad. It has to do with your faith because of God's grace. That's it.

Being born of the flesh as a descendant of Adam makes us unrighteous sinners, but the good news is that our unrighteousness is not dependent on *how much* we've sinned. If one person (without Jesus) only sins one time in their entire life, they are just as unrighteous as a person (without Jesus) who sins thousands of times. Why is that good news? Because that means it isn't about what we do. We can't make ourselves more righteous by trying not to sin, which is why we need Jesus. He is the only one that can fix our situation. Not only are we born anew in Him as a righteous child of God, but because of our new birth, our sins are forgiven, we are made alive in Jesus, are no longer separated from God, and we inherit eternal life. Wow!

Take note that it didn't take the Jewish law to make us unrighteous. If we became unrighteous by breaking the law of Moses, then we might think we are able to become righteous by obeying it. Since we are born into unrighteousness apart from the law, we cannot make ourselves righteous by obeying the law. In fact, *we* can't make ourselves righteous at all!

Isn't that great news? It reminds me of when Jesus said we could rest in Him. We don't have to work to become righteous. We can rest. He is our rest, every moment of every day. He is our Savior.

I pay for the membership to a popular online shopping site. I pay for it because I love the free shipping and it also allows me to donate a small amount of each purchase to a charity I love. Recently I realized there are several other membership benefits I hadn't been taking advantage of, like getting a couple free e-books per month, having the option of trying on stuff before I commit to purchasing it, and getting a discount on certain video games. I may or may not ever use these other benefits, but I haven't *yet* because I didn't know they existed.

Likewise, there was a time when I didn't know about certain unused benefits as a member of the family of God. It wasn't until about fifteen years ago that I was made aware of them. My hubby pastor, Phil, taught me about these awesome advantages that are given to us over and above our new righteousness.

When teaching about this topic he would say, "It's like God is saying, 'Hey righteous one, now I'm going to give you the real goods of this life.'"

As if eternity and forgiveness of sins aren't wonderful enough, God gives us these gifts before we get to enter time without end.

God's radical grace gives us multiple gifts – "membership benefits." For one, we are set free from everything that holds us back from loving others and being authentically us. Also, it provides us an underlying joy that is not based on the rollercoaster of this life but instead based on the relationship we have with our God through Jesus. He makes us alive in Him. We are awakened from the deadness of this world into a life that reflects that new joy.

We are living in a world that tells us we are supposed to be happy, but too often our happiness comes and goes with our circumstances. Many of us are told we are not good enough in school, work, church, or at home. We end up focusing on our failures rather than God's love. Additionally, we are reminded to love others, but we all struggle with doing so. Why can't we truly have joy, accept ourselves for who we are, live in God's grace, and genuinely love others?

Because the true and complete definition of God's grace is rarely talked about, so it isn't understood. Once you do understand it fully, you won't struggle to have joy, accept your authentic self, live fully in His grace, and love others deeply. In fact, you will not be able to contain your love for others.

God's grace is radical and revolutionary and thus produces radical changes in our lives when we learn how to embrace it. When we understand who we are in Jesus, we know we are both lovable and loved, as well as enjoyable and enjoyed. We don't have to hide who we are or hide from God. We are freed to be authentically us, authentically love, and authentically experience joy no matter what the world throws at us. And these are the things that are eternal and spiritual that create life in the dead world around us.

When we think about the fall of man and our need for a Savior, most of us are usually thinking about our ultimate salvation. God's grace is about more than our trip into heaven and eternity, it is about the here and now. It is about this moment. His grace is not only for us, but it also flows from us because we are made righteous and alive in Him. His grace is about life, love, mercy, forgiveness, joy, encouragement, peace, faith, rest, service, and everything that describes our new life in Christ.

I know many people who are struggling for the freedom, joy, and authenticity I am talking about. Maybe you are too. When you found yourself in need of saving, and God answered, He lifted you up, gave you a new identity, handed you the real goods of this life, and desires for you to be blessed beyond what you ever imagined. We are going to explore these additional blessings Jesus has offered you as we discover God's radical grace together. We need grace, not only for our ultimate salvation, but also for today.

When I was hanging on for dear life literally by my fingernails, I was in desperate need of a savior. My little six-year-old self didn't have any clue as to how true that was. Now I understand that God knew, and He sent Jesus to rescue me. He didn't just pull me out of a difficult situation, though, He bled for me. That is radical grace.

CHAPTER 5

The Promise

It's been about grace all along.

I was born with scoliosis. The curve and twist in my spine are in the lower part of my back. When I was born the doctors told my mother that it was so bad that I wouldn't ever be able to have children because the stress on my back from the weight of the baby would be too much for my body to bear. When I was three, the doctor gave me exercises to do at home and suggested I be put in gymnastics so I could strengthen my back muscles. He said that everything I did to the right side, I should do to the left. Right cartwheel. Left cartwheel. Right round-off. Left round-off. This balanced approach would facilitate strengthening both sides of my back. It wouldn't necessarily allow me to bear children, but it would help me deal with my birth defect.

At a young age I knew that I wanted to be a mommy someday. I was saddened that the doctor said I probably wouldn't be able to have children. To make me feel better and offer a solution, my mom talked to me about adoption. She would tell me of all the beautiful aspects of adoption.

"If you adopt a child, you get to give them a home and a family they need," she would say.

She told me about my cousins who were adopted and reassured me that I didn't have to go childless if my future husband and I wanted children. That was all I needed. I just knew that someday I would adopt.

Looking back at how God prepared my heart for adoption I realize that it wasn't only a preparation, but a promise. It was a way He put that beautiful act of love in my soul, to keep for revelation later in life.

Meanwhile, I continued my exercise regimen. I practically grew up in gyms! I ended up able to do back flips, walkovers on the beam, and splits in all the ways that would make you cringe.

When I was sixteen, my doctor informed me that because of my efforts I would likely be able to have a child when I was ready. I might, he warned, be restricted to a wheelchair during the pregnancy, but I should be able to carry a child. *A* child. One pregnancy.

Fast forward to when I was twenty-two, married to my beloved, Phil, and pregnant. I was managing the physical strain. I wasn't in a wheelchair, but I couldn't do much. Phillip willingly did all the housework for about six months. He's a hero.

After our son was born, we decided to try one more time since I hadn't had to use a wheelchair the last time. We didn't feel we were tempting fate, but that we were trusting God. We had our daughter two years after our son. It was difficult as well, but I did it! I knew I was done though and couldn't risk a third pregnancy. We made the choice to make that impossible.

But there was that promise I had from God years ago. I knew in my innermost being that God had a child for us out there somewhere that wasn't going to come from our DNA.

Six years later our cherished daughter was born, and we picked her up a month after her birth. She is every bit as much of a blessing as our older two children. We are so thankful to our Father who fulfills His promises. Adoption is a beautiful thing.

God promised me an adopted child when I was just old enough to dream about my future life as a mommy. When we had our son and daughter, their births didn't negate God's promise of an adopted child. They were altogether a different deal we had with God. He provided us the opportunity to have our biological children. Then, we also received the blessing of our youngest daughter through the long-promised adoption.

This story of ours reminds me of God's promise of the New Covenant.

God loves people so much that He wants us to be with Him forever. While we are born into sin and death through the "Fall," He knows there is nothing we can do to become righteous or avoid death on our own. Therefore, God put a plan in place. He promised to fix humanity's situation through grace.

In Genesis we read about a conversation Abram (later called Abraham) had with God. God came to him in a vision and promised him an heir. At the time, Abram and his wife were very old and had yet to have any children. God told Abram that he would have a son, Isaac, and through that son, God planned to bless the entire world. Abram believed that God would fulfill His promise to him. God accounted, or credited, Abram with righteousness because of his faith.

So how will all the nations of the earth be blessed through Abraham's son? Jesus. Jesus is a direct descendant of Abraham through Isaac. Through Jesus' death and resurrection, people of all nations are blessed. The promise was that Jesus would come to save, by grace, those who would put their faith in His righteousness. Jesus is the substance of the promise God had made to Abraham. This is the Gospel of Grace!

We see that God shared the gospel promise to Abraham thousands of years before Jesus came. Abraham believed in this good news message and because of his faith, he was given the righteousness of God and was saved. Abraham's receiving of God's righteousness was a foreshadowing of our receiving the righteousness of Jesus through faith in Him. We are adopted children of God! What a glorious thing to be called a child of God and heir to the promise of the Gospel of Grace!

Four hundred thirty years after that conversation with Abraham, God gave the law to the Jewish nation. It is important to note that when the law came along, it didn't nullify, or negate, the previous promise of the still future gospel promise that God had made to Abraham.

Why is this such an important point? Because the law was never intended to replace or terminate the promised gospel, nor to be infused into the gospel. The pledged Gospel of Grace was put in place *before* the law and has been the underlying message of God from the beginning of creation. It's been about grace all along. The law is simply a parenthetical placed within the timeline of humanity between the promise of the Gospel and the advent of the Gospel. The law had a purpose, for sure, but obeying it wasn't to remain as an objective once the promise was fulfilled. This is key to appreciating God's truly wonderful and radical grace.

The law also doesn't supersede the grace deal we have with God in the New Covenant. The law is simply what God had for the nation of Israel for a specified period between the initial promise and when the promise was completed. It held a space until the new deal based on faith was initiated. The law reveals the great contrast between trying to become righteous by our own efforts, and the beauty of becoming righteous by the grace of God through faith in Jesus.

At a young age God promised me I would someday have an adopted child, and He fulfilled that promise when I was thirty-two. Phil and I remained faithful that God would complete His promise to us. Having our other two children prior to our second daughter's adoption didn't nullify that promise.

Likewise, Abraham was faithful that God would fulfill the promise made to him. When God gave the Jewish nation their law, that didn't nullify the pending promise of a yet future Savior and the new deal He would make with His followers.

People often ask, "So, what about the law? Why did God give it to us if we aren't supposed to make it an important part of our faith?"

Paul answers that very question for us. I'll share his answer with you in the next chapter. We will see the reason for the law and our relationship to it as a faithful follower of Jesus. God's plan has always been to save us through our faith in Jesus. We are not saved, nor made righteous through obedience to the law or good deeds, but through His radical grace.

CHAPTER 6

The Law

The law reveals the need for grace.

There was no speed limit sign as I exited my new neighborhood in New Mexico to go to my job as a pizza deliverywoman. In Colorado, where I learned to drive, the speed limit of a residential area was 30 miles per hour so I assumed that was what I should go in my new town. I was trying not to be late for work and I pushed my speed to 34 mph. I knew I was pushing it a little, but 4 mph over the speed limit, that isn't too bad, right? My speedometer could be off by that much.

I was driving along happily listening to the radio when I heard a siren and saw flashing lights in the mirrors. I pulled over and the officer informed me that I was going 35mph in a 25-mph zone. What? 35? I don't think so, but more importantly, it's a 25-mph zone? *So that's the speed limit!* What could I say? I was caught and I should have known better. I took the ticket and went to work ...going one mile per hour slower than the speed limit through the rest of the neighborhood.

Later, as I slung hot pizzas into my car, I thought about how surprised I was to know that I had broken the law by ten (nine) miles per hour! One minute I thought of myself as a pretty good person, and the next minute I realized I was a *law breaker*! Knowing the law made my sin apparent because only then did I know that I had broken it.

I know, this isn't really a huge deal in the vast history of all sin, but this scenario speaks to why God gave the nation of Israel their law. Israel needed a measuring stick, a clear speed limit sign, to really understand how far they had strayed from God. That ruler wasn't the path to righteousness, just revelation.

The covenant God made with the Israelite nation through Moses from atop Mt. Sinai required them to obey His law. It was an "if-then" deal. God's actions and responses were based on their obedience. *If* they obeyed God's commands, *then* He promised He would be an enemy to their enemies, make them a special people and a kingdom of priests.

If you have read the Old Testament, you know the nation of Israel didn't hold up their end of the deal. Why? Because they couldn't. After all, they were born of Adam. They were born unrighteous. It is impossible to perfectly fulfill the law when you are unrighteous.

So, why did God give them the law? Surely, He would have known they couldn't meet their end of the deal.

Yes, He knew.

Like my incident with the speeding ticket, Paul tells us the law was given so sin would appear as sinful. I had no clue I was breaking the law, or sinning, until the officer told me the law. Knowing the law made my sin more obviously sinful. Likewise, the law was given so the Jewish people would be aware of their sin through their breaking of it.

The law serves to reveal to us that we are sinful and unrighteous and that we need Jesus. We need grace.

As a kid I didn't know Jesus. I knew of Him, but we didn't go to church or read the Bible. Maybe Mom read it, but if she did, she read it privately. She would speak of Jesus when she demanded that I forgive my brother for something he did to me, but otherwise His name wasn't brought up much. We celebrated Jesus' birth at Christmas, but I didn't know the true meaning of Easter. I thought there might be a God, so I used to talk to Him at night while in my bed, especially when I was scared. I'd always start off by saying, "God, if you are there..."

I wonder how life would have been different had I truly known Him. I was sexually abused as a very young child by one man in my life and then again by another when I was eleven. Some of the consequences of this abuse was that it made me feel dirty, used, and afraid of people. I felt worthless. Often this type of abuse either drives people to the gutter of despair or in the opposite direction toward polishing themselves up on the outside to gain approval from those around them. I mostly chose the latter. The despair part still lived on the inside, but most people didn't know that. I was able to fake my confidence. It was like I was two different people; the hurt one internally and the one who looked on the outside like she had it all together.

Striving to find value in myself, I tried to do everything well. First, I was a good gymnast. After I cracked a rib and couldn't sit up easily for two months, I quit gymnastics and started playing the clarinet and saxophone. I drove myself to be the best so I could win awards, receive compliments, and stroke my wounded ego. I tried to always obey my parents. In school I obeyed my teachers and got good grades. I placed in the science fair. I was named student of the year by the Lions Club. I made drum major. I was yelling to the world, "SEE, I AM WORTH SOMETHING!"

But inside, I still felt dirty, used, afraid, and worthless. No matter how much I achieved, or studiously wore those goody two-shoes, it didn't help. It didn't help because trying to be good couldn't make me whole or healed.

When I was sixteen, Phillip led me to the Lord. I understood the basics of the Gospel; that I was a sinner, and I needed a Savior. Understanding that I was a transgressor of the law brought me to Christ, and I was hopeful about the possibility of not having to try so hard to prove my value.

As a new Christian I was taught to try to avoid sin so I could become more like Jesus and a better person. I had learned to be pretty good at being good, so that mission sounded doable. I approached my relationship with Jesus the same way I had approached my life prior to receiving Him, but this time it was for God, not the people around me. This time my efforts would actually clean me up, so I thought. In my mind, it was a righteous aim, and since being good was a familiar task to me, I settled into that life for many years. I thought, *maybe if I do good for God, I will finally feel okay.* Trying to be good, though, just made me feel more like a failure because I couldn't avoid sin. I still felt dirty, used, afraid, and worthless.

And it got worse! The more I tried to be perfect the more I became angry, judgmental, frustrated, and self-righteous. By the time I was in my thirties I had run out of steam. I was tired of struggling. No matter how hard I tried and how much I prayed, I always ended up repeating the things I thought I had conquered. It was like I was on a hamster wheel, and I couldn't get off. I remember envisioning crawling into God's really big lap, cuddling up, and simply telling Him, "I give up."

That was the beginning of my journey toward healing. I had received salvation by faith, but it wasn't until I gave up on trying to become righteous by my own efforts that I was truly drawn to a deep relationship with Jesus. His grace drew me in.

My dear friend, what about you? Maybe you struggled to develop your self-worth. Maybe your story is similar in some ways. Do you feel unworthy or unclean because of things people have done to you? Maybe you have done things that haunt you and drive you to thinking you are unworthy of God's love. Perhaps you haven't experienced anything so traumatic, but you still strive ceaselessly to be a better Christian or become more sinless, and you feel like you just can't succeed. No matter what drives you, my heart breaks for you, and I am here to remind you that you are not alone; you can stop working so hard. You can cuddle up in God's lap and tell Him you quit.

Now that Jesus has come, no one is bound by the law and that is one of the great blessings we receive when we put our trust in Him. Like the nation of Israel, our righteousness can't come by the law. The writer of Hebrews tells us the law was ineffective at making people perfect. With or without the law, everyone is a sinner and falls short of God's glorious righteousness.

So, how did Jesus fix this problem? How are we freed from the law?

First, because Christ was able to fulfill the law. We are told this fact in the Book of Matthew. Jesus obeyed it perfectly; He was without sin. Only He could satisfy its requirements. I know you've been taught this concept because we all have been taught it. So, why do we hear this and still think we are going to become sinless somehow? We set lofty goals for ourselves knowing we can never achieve them. No wonder we end up with negative self-talk and discouraged, guilty souls.

And second, because Christ fulfilled the law, He released us from it. Remember, obeying the Old Testament law was a requirement of the deal God made with the Jewish nation. It is part of the Old Covenant. That covenant has been fulfilled by Jesus. It is over. We are all released from its conditions through His fulfilling of it perfectly. In the Book of Colossians, Paul discusses this. He tells us that Jesus nailed to the cross the written requirements, or law, that we couldn't accomplish anyway.

You don't need to spend your time trying to obey either the Old Testament laws or any man-made rules to make yourself better or to avoid sin. You are wasting your time focused on something Jesus already did for you. Please don't miss the beauty of the New Covenant and the life Jesus afforded you through His death and resurrection. As a participant in the New Covenant, the goal isn't to avoid sin. We simply can't do it. The fact is, we are so free in Jesus that we *can* "go around sinning all the time" and still be forgiven. Let's be honest, we do! That is why God's grace is so radical.

As a child of God, though, you know that isn't what Jesus had in mind when He freed you. What did He tell you to do? He told you to love Him and love others. It isn't about avoiding sin; it is about love. There is no law against loving others.

As faithful followers of Christ let's be careful not to try to intertwine the Old Covenant with the New Covenant. That doesn't work. It's impossible. Jesus is the embodiment of the promised eternal covenant that God made with Abraham. This new deal is much better for us than the old one. When Jesus brought in the New

Covenant, He not only brought His forgiveness for our transgression of the Old Testament law, but He brought His righteousness to us as well. We don't have to work for it. We simply believe that Jesus' righteousness is good enough to make us righteous. That is the beauty of the gospel of God's radical grace.

If grace through faith in Jesus was the plan preached and promised to Abraham, which was not only given before the law of Moses, but it also has nothing to do with the law, how has the law garnered such a prominent place in our faith? Christianity has close ties to the Jewish religion, and many teach that the law of the Old Testament is the foundation upon which we are to build our relationship with God. Sadly, in today's Christian culture, fulfilling the law is a main point of many teachings. But what does that really mean? Most of us aren't trying to avoid eating shellfish or offering a sacrifice for our sins. Well, I am avoiding the shellfish, actually, but not because of the Old Testament law.

If it isn't *really* about fulfilling the Old Testament laws, what are these teachings implying? It seems there is an unspoken Christian code that we all assume we understand, but no one ever really defines. This unspoken code of conduct is not legalism, in that we aren't trying to fulfill the Mosaic Law, but it has, however, the spirit of legalism. It is a pressure to perform; to do good and not do bad. I will explore this idea further in chapter eight.

The law showed the world that we are incapable of being perfectly righteous by our own efforts. It revealed to us that we need a Savior. Trying to fulfill the law serves you no purpose. God wrote His law on your heart, so you have that as a compass and inspiration as you walk in the Spirit, but once you receive Jesus as your Savior, you are not under the law, but under God's radical grace.

CHAPTER 7

The New Covenant

Amazing grace breaks chains.

Amazing grace
How sweet the sound
That saved a wretch like me
I once was lost, but now I'm found
Was blind, but now I see

John Newton's *Amazing Grace* speaks to those of us who have experienced spiritual blindness, but also know what it is to see. These familiar lyrics have been sung for over two hundred years by people of faith.

This recently added chorus is particularly inspiring.

My chains are gone
I've been set free
My God, my Savior has ransomed me
And like a flood, His mercy rains
Unending love, amazing grace[4]

This is a fitting addition, as Newton understood both sides of the chains. He had not only been a slave trader, but he had also been chained up himself. He knew the Savior had set him free from his wretched past and he danced in the rain of mercy God had for him.

At our little church in the mountains of New Mexico, we did some unorthodox things on some Sunday mornings. We had a dog, Star, who frequented our meetings and who often barked right at the time Phil was making a powerful point. Tissue paper butterflies hung from the ceiling one Sunday to punctuate Phil's sermon about being made new in Christ. Another time we had a net full of little balloons that we dropped on our beloved friends below to make a point about the probability of Jesus fulfilling the prophecies about Him. One thing that blessed me greatly was our worship dance team. I think they, too, danced in the rain of God's mercy. It was always a beautiful blessing to worship with them on those Sunday mornings.

I found myself in tears one morning while the dancers were worshipping to Chris Tomlin's version of *Amazing Grace*. By this time in my life God had brought me through much healing, but I still felt I was in the chains of my past. Not the chains of my sin. I had accepted Christ's forgiveness for my own sin, but specifically, the chains that I received from the men who had abused me. What they had done to me was still affecting me and my relationship with Phillip.

God took the opportunity to speak to me during the chorus that morning. I realized Jesus wants to set me free by His amazing grace! He had *already* ransomed me. My chains were *already* broken because Jesus had set me free. I just needed to realize that fact, shake them off, let them drop to the ground, and step away.

That was the moment I recognized I had been denying myself the complete goodness of the New Covenant
and God's grace. I understood that His grace was not
only for the chains *my sin* had put me in, but it was also
for the sins of those who had hurt me and the chains *they*
had put me in. The New Covenant Gospel of Grace is
amazing!

We read in the Book of Hebrews that Jesus is the mediator of the New Covenant. It also says that the New
Covenant is a better covenant than the old one. Remember, the New Covenant was promised to Abraham well
before the Jewish law ever existed, and upon Jesus' death
and resurrection, it was set in motion. The New Covenant not only preceded the Mosaic Covenant, but it
supersedes it. I love that the writer of Hebrews calls
Jesus' ministry a "more excellent ministry."

Newton's lyrics reflect the results of Jesus' excellent
ministry. If you are struggling to relate to Newton's
response to the Gospel, I suggest that you keep reading
and allow God's radical grace to rain down on you.

So, how is Jesus' ministry more excellent?

In the last chapter I talked about the Mosaic Covenant
being an "if-then" arrangement. *If* the Jewish nation
obeyed the law, *then* the LORD God would protect them
and make them a special kingdom of priests. That deal
was about the nation of Israel being obedient to God

through the laws He gave them, and that obedience held certain consequences that they would receive if they obeyed, and other consequences if they disobeyed. Sadly, but not surprisingly, the Jewish nation couldn't fulfill the *if* part because of their inherent unrighteousness, and they suffered for it.

It is worth noting, salvation has always been about faith in Jesus. We can see God's plan of radical grace from Eden to Mt. Moriah to Golgotha, where the cross of Christ was erected.

Keeping that big picture in mind, we can correctly see that the Old Covenant is an example for us that we cannot obtain righteousness on our own. That is why the Israelites had to continuously, year after year, bring animals to sacrifice at the Temple to cover their sins. The law reveals to us that we are sinners and in need of a Savior. The apostle Paul explains to us that with the law, sin abounded, and where sin abounded, grace abounded much more.

The new and better covenant is an "I will" deal. There is no "if-then." It is a one-sided pledge by God. There is no requirement for us to fulfill or do anything, we simply step into that deal by simply having faith that Jesus fulfilled the Old Covenant. His sacrificial death and miraculous resurrection were the beginning of the New Covenant. God's new promise declares that because we are unrighteous, He will take care of that unrighteous-ness so we can be together both now, and forever. This new deal is about the free gift of eternal life, but it is also about a new life now that doesn't require us to fulfill "our side" of the contract. Jesus took care of everything. That is why the New Covenant, which is for both the Jews and the Gentiles, is better and "more excellent!"

God says through the prophet Jeremiah (31:31-34) that when we put our faith in the righteousness of Jesus, He will do the following:

- *I will* put My law in their minds and write it on their hearts
- *I will* be their God, and they shall be My people
- *I will* forgive their iniquity
- *I will* be merciful to their unrighteousness
- their sin and lawless deeds *I will* remember no more

Notice the promise of the New Covenant makes no mention of obeying a set of laws. Once we are in Christ, God does the work.

Paul underscores this argument in his letter to the Romans. He says that even before the law of Moses was given to the nation of Israel, sin was in the world, but, he says, sin wasn't imputed because there was no law. This is a critical truth to understand. *Impute* means to *put something on someone's account* or *attribute, assign* or *credit* to someone. So, from the time of Adam to Moses, although sin was in the world, it wasn't imputed or held against people. It wasn't attributed to or assigned to the people who lived during that period because the law hadn't been given to them yet.

We can grasp and hold tight some important truths here. First, Paul says sin was present, which confirms that we are born unrighteous sinners and we don't need the law to make that true.

Second, those who lived during the time between Adam and Moses didn't have the law, so sin wasn't put on their account. When there was no law, there was no law to break, so God didn't keep track of their sin. He didn't impute it.

Paul is making sure we understand the relationship that sin has with the law because that is important in our understanding of our situation as New Covenant believers. Jesus died and rose again to take away the requirement to fulfill the law, through finalizing the Old Covenant, and initiating the New Covenant. Where there is no law, sin is not imputed, because there is no transgression of the law.

When I first got this as I was reading my Bible, I said out loud, "Ohhhhhhh, wow! That makes sense." I realized that because I have faith in Jesus, God doesn't record my sins in some big book somewhere that He can refer to when I stand before Him one day. My sins are not put on my account. That is what forgiveness is all about. That is radical grace.

This was mind blowing to me! Seeing the perspective of my sin while in Christ versus my sin while under the law freed me from thinking I had to strive to perfect my sinful flesh to get God's approval and to be a better Christian. Jesus took care of my sin. This concept helped me to know the tremendous value and precious blessing of the New Covenant.

There is something else that I had to get to fully receive the blessings of the Gospel of Grace. In Christ, sin is not imputed to us, but there is something that is. Recall that God accounted Abraham's faith as righteousness when he believed that God would bless the world through one of his descendants. The word *accounted* in that verse is the same Hebrew word *imputed* I just talked about. God credited Abraham with righteousness because of his faith, and likewise, He credits us with His righteousness because of our faith.

My friend, this is such a crucial point. Abraham lived over 400 years before Moses and the law, and he lived 2,000 years before Jesus came, but God imputed His righteousness to him. He made him righteous. Why? Because Abraham believed and trusted in God. That's it! Faith! It has always been about faith and always will be about faith.

The pact with Moses was about obedience to the law, but the pact with Abraham was all about faith. Abraham had faith in God, and it was about a Savior who would come for those who had faith in Him. Remember, those of us who are in Christ because of our faith in Him are imputed His righteousness through His radical grace.

In 2019, I updated our guest bathroom in our farmhouse and bought a little wooden sign that has a funny saying on it.

"You never know what you have until it's gone. Toilet paper, for instance."

At the time I didn't fully grasp the truth of that little sign. Then the coronavirus pandemic hit the next year and people inexplicably started hoarding toilet paper. Not only that, but in the early days of the pandemic, I couldn't even purchase paper towels or boxes of tissue unless I happened to be at the store when they were unloading the rare delivery truck. Otherwise, the supply would be bought up immediately.

Like many people, I had neglected to appreciate how nice it was to always have basic household supplies available. I pray I never do that again!

Similarly, the New Covenant is not appreciated for what it is. Part of the problem is that many people try to fit it into the Old Covenant where it doesn't belong. That would be like trying to merge two different contracts or the wills of two different deceased people.

The Bible tells us that the prophets investigated the message of grace and even the angels desired to look into such things. I imagine they were intrigued about it because although they didn't get to participate in the New Covenant, it sounded amazing to them. Unlike the sudden scarcity of toilet paper that caught us off guard, we know the basic beauty of the Gospel. However, we can't see its complete splendor when we try to place it inside of the Old Covenant. We don't even realize we are doing it, but when we do, we are missing out on the fullness of the blessings Jesus has for us in this new deal.

This concept reminds me of the parable of the wineskins. I must admit, I didn't understand this parable until I understood grace. Jesus told us that when you use an old wineskin for new wine, the wineskin breaks, and the wine pours out, but when you use a new wineskin for new wine, both are maintained. During His last Passover, Jesus called His cup of wine the blood of the covenant. The wine symbolizes His blood which represents His grace through His sacrifice for our salvation. The wineskins represent the covenants. Jesus was telling us that we cannot put the grace of Jesus' Gospel into the Old Covenant. It must be kept in the New Covenant context to be preserved. Grace is not grace if we try to put it into an "if-then" or work-reward system like the agreement God had with the nation of Israel. It can only be maintained if we keep it pure and within the context of the New Covenant. Luke alluded to the fact that this would be difficult for some to accept by noting that no one desires new wine after having drunk the old stuff.

When we lose sight of God's amazing grace, we lose the beauty of life that Jesus has offered us. We not only become blind to what God has done for us, but because of that, we stop living in the blessings of His grace. We stop appreciating what we have. We don't think about it, just like we used to not think about toilet paper.

Praise God His grace isn't going to disappear from our lives, so we don't need to fear the experience that we won't realize what we had until it is gone. But I would like to encourage you to take a new look at His grace and renew your appreciation for it. His grace is amazing. Many of us have been forgiven much and we are so very thankful. I know you acknowledge His grace in your life. That is a beautiful thing.

Going forward, I hope you can see that His grace is more abundant and radical than you even know in this moment. I am so excited to share with you some amazing revelations God has given me that have loosed me from my chains and allowed me to dance in the rain of His amazing radical grace.

My chains are gone
I've been set free
My God, my Savior has ransomed me
And like a flood, His mercy rains
Unending love, amazing grace[4]

CHAPTER 8

The CODE

Grace is limitless.

B efore I understood God's grace and how truly
radical it is, I lived a life in the chains of legalism.
As a result of the abuse that I had endured as a
child, I lacked any understanding of self-value. Like I
have shared, in response to that belief I worked hard to
be a good child and student. That perpetuated into my
adulthood, and it changed from trying to be good for my
parents and teachers to trying to be good for my new
daddy, God.

When I was a young Christian, the churches I attended leaned toward legalism, which fed my need to
impress God. I was confused, though, because we were
told we are to obey a combination of Old Testament laws
and modern Christian rules. Some of the laws we were to
obey were the Ten Commandments, but other laws such
as celebrating the Feasts of God and not getting a tattoo
were ignored. It was strange to me that Christianity was
selective or arbitrary in the laws that it chose to honor.

Other rules that weren't specifically from the Jewish
law were also talked about as being our duty to obey.

There are two kinds of rules in this category: those that are created from verses in the New Testament writings and those that are constructed from modern culture.

When you read the New Testament you will find many statements, suggestions, and encouragements by the writers that have been transformed into "commands" in the Christian faith. For example, in Hebrews chapter ten the author encourages us not to forsake getting together with fellow believers because when we do, we can exhort each other to walk in love. This encouragement has been turned into a legalistic command to go to church. What was written as a beautiful inspiration to Jesus followers to gather has become a guilt producing obligation. Going to church and fellowshipping with others is a beautiful thing, but once you make it a rule, you attach shame and condemnation if someone doesn't measure up. I lived by this "command." I went to church dutifully, and when I didn't, I felt like I was being a bad Christian.

Certain cultural rules were pressed upon us as well, like rules about holidays. For example, we shouldn't say "Happy Easter," we should say, "Happy Resurrection Day." Christmas trees are pagan, so if you put one up, you were walking a very thin line, and let's not even talk about Halloween! We had to be careful because hobbies, sports teams, or our nice car might become our idols. If you are overweight, that means you are gluttonous and if you are wealthy, that means you are greedy. You must read your Bible and pray every day for a certain amount of time and if you ever went to the wedding of a gay couple, you must be a heathen. There were rules about television and movies, politics, clothing, and language. The list was extensive. Although the list of "commandments" and "rules" we were taught to obey was not necessarily set in stone, pun intended, we were to follow them, nonetheless.

This Christian lifestyle seemed spiritual and righteous to me, so I obeyed to impress God and everyone around me. I needed to prove that I was good. I obeyed *for* righteousness' sake.

My poor children. For many years we didn't have TV and when we did have TV, they were strictly limited in what they could watch. These weren't just common-sense restrictions like no rated R movies, but ridiculous restrictions of innocent cartoons and movies simply because they were too worldly or "might influence my kids to rebel." They still tease me about this to this day. I avoided drinking wine and eating pork. I felt shameful if a cuss word ever escaped my lips. Santa didn't come to our house and there were many other *don'ts* and *shoulds* I obeyed. The constraints were numerous. Yet in the end, all it gave me was a good dose of self-righteousness.

With the planting of self-righteousness in the fertile soil of my legalistic heart, a tree of judgmentalism grew big and strong. When I failed at obedience, I felt ashamed, and once shame set in, I needed to counteract that shame with comparison to others so I could feel better about my own failures and faults. I would look for others that *weren't behaving as well as I was* so I could feel better about myself.

Despite the so-called promise of righteousness, I was miserable. My legalistic approach to life not only hindered my relationships with God and others, but it kept me from walking in the freedom that God's grace had afforded me.

Your experience may not be as extreme as mine, but I'd bet you've encountered legalism in some form or another. In the last few years, I have heard and seen many social media posts, sermons, sayings, and song lyrics that have the same spirit of legalism. This version doesn't focus on specific edicts and laws per se, but it generally emphasizes working on your sin and being a better person through doing "good." It is hidden in the things that we hear that we should do more of, less of, or better.

Often, the term used in this type of legalism is *obedience*, but rarely do I hear people define that obedience. What does that look like? What am I supposed to do or not do? I think you can agree with me, the word *obedience* is often used as a placeholder for legalism. The problem with this type of legalism is its vagueness makes it more confusing and less likely anyone will question its validity because, after all, we are supposed to do good as a child of God, right? Folks just talk about obedience, hammering home the idea that you aren't righteous enough, so do better.

If you Google "obedience to God" or ask people to define it, you get several different responses. Some people give specifics, saying obedience to God means to obey the Ten Commandments or other Old Testament laws. Others turn New Testament encouragements into rules to obey or make up rules about what we can and can't do like I shared with you about my early experiences in church. Whatever the rules that are given, the basic message is that we should try to avoid sin, "do good," and don't "do bad." Obedience, or disobedience, is determined by whether what we do is *good* versus if what we do is *bad*. If we read our Bible, chalk one in the *good* column. If we say a cuss word, mark the *bad* column. Serve at the community kitchen = good. Yell at your wife = bad. Good, bad, good, good, bad. It's an equation we are trying desperately to keep weighted on the good side, and if it is, we can say we are "obedient to God."

For my purpose in this book, I will hereafter refer to this concept as the CODE; The Christian Obedience/Disobedience Equation.

Please note that I am not saying doing good things is a bad idea. The point is though, our relationship with Jesus isn't about learning to be obedient and striving for our good behavior to outweigh our bad behavior, it is about learning to love one another, have compassion, empathy, and understanding with one another. In Jesus, the motivation for what we do is love, not to avoid doing bad things.

God needed to establish the law in order for us to understand its limitations and its contrast with grace. We cannot understand grace unless we understand that grace took care of our failure to love. In that grace, God made us righteous and gave us what we need to love Him and love others.

We should look at the law and the failure of the Jewish nation to perfectly obey it as an example and warning for us. God showed us through that example that making obedience the point didn't work. But if He had just started with grace and never showed us that contrast, we wouldn't understand the beauty of His grace, we wouldn't recognize our transgressions, and we wouldn't seek the God who paid for them. But remaining in that system keeps us from doing what God has always wanted for us, which is to do much more than simply to obey, it is to love. So, why are going back to that same method and just updating the set of rules for modern times?

If you feel obligated to obey, pressured to perform, or guilty if you fail to achieve perfect behavior, you are striving in your flesh to obey instead of freely walking according to the Spirit by God's grace in love. We have been given everything we need to live our lives in the righteousness that Jesus has already given us. In that righteousness, we can do great things for the kingdom of God and for others, but it's neither a "should" nor an "ought to," it's a "get to," and in fact, it's a *desire to* because of God's love, and that is a huge difference.

This form of legalism is like a virus. It spreads insidiously, leaving a devastating wake, and it is working its way through the Christian body. It is limiting and weakening the faith of God's children and preventing people from coming to Jesus as well. Paul the apostle addressed it extensively in his writings, yet, sadly, 2,000 years later the virus lives on. Why? Because legalism is both familiar to us and subtle, so it is easily spread. If we aren't on the lookout for it, we miss it entirely. In a later chapter, I will give you specific keys that will help you to spot and avoid legalism.

See, our society is based on a work-reward system, and we are born into that system. From the time we are infants we are taught that bad behavior equals punishment, and good behavior and hard work equals reward. Our educational, occupational, and even societal systems all work this way. That is how the world works and that is what we know.

The Christian faith often approaches God as if He partakes in that same system. Our familiarity with this work-reward method causes us to settle easily into a similar legalistic approach to our faith. Our natural instinct is to do things *for* something. Modern Christian culture suggests that we need to be "good" to become more like Jesus, which translates to us trying to become more righteous, holy, or so God won't be disappointed in us. We are encouraged to do good *for* righteousness, not because we are *already* righteous and can do good for others while living in that righteousness.

This CODE is that form of legalism. Why? Because it encourages doing good for the sake of obedience, which really means *for* righteousness, rather than for love *in* righteousness.

There is a great scripture in 2 Timothy that helps us to understand this concept. Let's look at it briefly.

*All Scripture is given by inspiration of God, and is profitable for doctrine, for reproof, for correction, for instruction **in** righteousness, that the man of God may be complete, thoroughly equipped for every good work.* (2 Ti 3:16-17, my emphasis added)

Notice it says that the Word of God is profitable, beneficial, or valuable for training *in* righteousness. It doesn't say *for* righteousness. It says *in*. We are already made righteous by Jesus so we can do great things in that righteousness. We don't have to work to become righteous. We don't have to be obedient to please God or to become more holy. He already made us holy, and He is already well pleased with us.

Paul addresses this legalistic idea at the beginning of the book of Galatians. After calling the Galatians foolish, he asked them if they thought they would become perfect by doing things in their flesh. It was a rhetorical question, of course, to make the point that they were striving in their flesh to do what Jesus had already done in the Spirit. Jesus removes us from the limits of our worldly flesh and places us into His spiritual kingdom. Paul says something interesting in his letter to the Romans.

But now we have been delivered from the law, having died to what we were held by, so that we should serve in the newness of the Spirit and not in the oldness of the letter. (Rom 7:6)

Paul was addressing Jewish people who were steeped in the old Jewish law, but the idea that he is talking about can be applied to the CODE too, as it pertains to rules that Christians place on themselves. Look at what Paul is saying. We are free to serve in the newness of the Spirit, not in the oldness of obeying a set of rules. Paul tells us why in his letter to the Corinthians.

*... our sufficiency is from God, who also made us sufficient as ministers of the new covenant, not of the letter but of the Spirit; for **the letter kills, but the Spirit gives life.*** (2 Co 3:5-6, my emphasis added)

Rules and laws limit us and kill all inspiration, creativity, and life that walking and living in the Spirit offers. We can obey a religious law or rule and not break it, but we can do so much more if we live and walk in the Spirit.

Following are two examples contrasting the legalistic CODE approach (*for* righteousness) with a spiritual approach (*in* righteousness).

We often hear that we should read our Bibles more. Not everyone defines "more," but some do. "You should read your Bible 30 minutes a day" or "Read your Bible, even if it is one verse, every morning." Sometimes there is no stated goal attached to these commands, but we all know that the CODE means we are to read our Bibles because that's what "good Christians" do. Be obedient.

First, just saying we "should" read every day auto-matically makes some people wince. Now it is a "have to" instead of a "get to."

Second, why limit it? If reading the Word is not pre-sented as a chore, a "should," or an "ought to," we might read our Bibles for more than 30 minutes per day or more than one verse at a time. When I "have to" read some-thing, I don't pay as close attention to it as when I am reading something I want to read. Wasn't that the case in school for most of us? If it was a subject we cared about, we paid attention, but if not, we weren't as involved in the subject matter. The same is true with the Bible. When we read with a "get to" attitude we want to hear what God has to say to us. We are not only more attentive to what we are reading, but because of that focus, we will understand it better and get much more out of our reading time than if we are apathetically polishing off a required amount of reading for the sake of checking it off our to-do list.

Reading plans work for people who are doing it as a "get to." However, they aren't so great for those who are doing the plan out of obedience, because if they miss a day, and they most likely will, they will hear that condemning voice in their head saying, "You failed," and they end up feeling ashamed.

Living *in* righteousness means we get to live by the Spirit. When we are inspired to read the Bible, we will dig in, and if we skip a day or twelve, there is no need to take on guilt because we know that reading our Bible doesn't affect how God feels about us, our righteousness, or our holiness. Living *in* righteousness is living in the freedom of His grace.

Living by the CODE limits our lives to legalistic obedience. Grace is the opposite of the CODE. Grace holds no expectation of work, performance, or obedience to receive God's blessings of His love, salvation, righteousness, and holiness.

The more we understand and accept the grace of God, the more we will live in that grace and give that grace to others. If we don't get grace, we aren't going to give it, and our lives will be wrapped up in unforgiveness, shame, guilt, depression, pride, or judgment. The CODE causes shame for those who don't measure up, which can produce an unforgiving heart and even drive people into depression. I know because I lived it. And for those rare few who manage to accomplish some obedience, pride can set in which leads to becoming judgmental. I lived this too. Either way, we compare ourselves to others to feel better about where we are on the quest to perfection.

Also, living by the CODE inhibits our authenticity. We feel we cannot be authentic with others because, if we fail at the task of obedience, we might be found out. People might realize what a wreck we are. So, we hide. In grace, we know we are accepted by God, we accept ourselves, and we do not need to wallow in the pool of shame when we fail. We can admit our failures and shortcomings and know that Jesus isn't surprised.

Weak faith is also a result of the CODE. We can't be sure of where we stand with God because we are playing a game of Chutes and Ladders where we climb up the ladders of success, then slide back down when we fail. When we don't know where we stand with God, we aren't sure we can trust Him. However, if we fully grasp His grace, then we know that we aren't even on that gameboard, and we can trust Him because we know His love and care for us is not based on what we do or don't do.

Living by the Spirit, however, is living in the freedom and beauty of God's radical grace. In that freedom, we can do anything and everything God has for us. The only "commands" Jesus gave us in the New Testament were to love God and love others and He said that if we love Him, we will do just that. He made it very simple for us, but if not taken in the Spirit, even these commands can be taken legalistically. For example, a church marquee might say, "How have you loved your neighbor lately?" This question places you right back on that gameboard.

It is radical that God decided to die for us, give us a new heart pre-packaged with His love, and sent His Spirit to help us spread that love to the world around us. In that grace we are unlimited in the ways we can love. No rules. No CODE. Simply love. That is radical grace.

CHAPTER 9

The Love of God

Grace is love given without the expectation of performance.

hillip's arms were wrapped around me firmly as he struggled to keep me from hurting myself any further. I had just gone into an uncontrollable fit of despair. I had hit myself anywhere I could: head, thighs, face. His arms were strong, holding me back from any movement, both protecting me from myself, and comforting me at the same time. As I struggled to choose between trying to escape my capture or surrendering to his embrace, the pain of the scratches I had inflicted on my arms prompted me to consider my decision carefully. The scent of his cologne was familiar as I burrowed my head into his chest listening to his heartbeat. The pounding in my head and the tears continually pouring down my face made my vision blurry. I just closed my eyes. I wished I could just vanish into thin air.

As I stood there, my mind struggled to reconcile the fact that Phillip loved me enough to fight for me, yet I felt so unworthy of that love. I was truly baffled.

During the first several years of our marriage my feelings of unworthiness drove me to moments like this far too often. These were the battles that Phillip and I went into together on a consistent basis. We weren't battling each other; we were battling the demons in my mind.

At a young age, my personal boundaries were invaded and trampled on. I was forced to experience things of a sexual nature before puberty and before I was old enough to understand what was going on. I was not able to control these situations and my second abuser won my silence for many years by threatening to hurt me if I told anyone.

I felt broken. I couldn't function like a normal, emotionally stable person. Being sexually abused multiple times as a young girl had devastating consequences for me, and my marriage. The emotional trauma had many ill effects, like becoming obsessive compulsive and agoraphobic (being fearful of crowds and people), and spawning episodes like the one I just described. But worse, it robbed me of my ability trust anyone, including God. Even after learning to trust Phillip enough to marry him, I didn't trust him with intimacy. I would have been perfectly happy to never have sex in my life.

That fact created quite the conundrum for me. See, I had spent my entire life trying to be obedient and follow the rules, to be the best at everything I did. From my delusional perspective, I believed I couldn't accomplish being a good wife if I didn't desire sex. Phil wasn't putting that pressure on me, I was. Outside of intimacy, I had been able to perform well, but this was something I couldn't accomplish. It was simply beyond my capabilities because of my trust issues. I grossly misunderstood what it meant to be a partner in a marriage. Because I was so familiar with working for approval and love, I assumed that was my job in my marriage. My inability to do the work of what I defined as a "good wife" made me think I was unworthy of the love that my husband said he had for me, and I didn't completely trust that what he said was even true. Shame overwhelmed me. I fell into my own trap that I had to perform well, do good, and make my hubby happy so that he would love me. And as a result, we were both miserable.

This cycle of misery went on for the first ten years of our marriage. Boy, did we struggle. Instead of intimacy being a blessing in our lives, it was often awkward and ended up with me, in tears saying, "I'm just broken."

But we also prayed. We sought God together over our seemingly impossible situation. Phillip recognized that whenever he suggested intimacy, I got upset. It was the very fact that intimacy had been *forced* on me as a child that made me resist any such act that didn't originate from within myself, and of my own will and desire, which rarely happened. At some point, God told Phillip to let go and just love me in grace without conditions. He asked Phillip to love me no matter what I did or didn't do.

Phillip's grace with me was the very thing that started us toward healing.

Phillip came to me one day and told me, "I love you no matter what you do or don't do. You don't have to do anything for me to make me love you. You could be in a body cast and never have sex with me again and I would still love you."

That single, loving statement and his commitment to it changed me. No more pressure to perform. No more expectations or judgment that I wasn't good enough. I was free to be who I was, the broken mess that he married. And I knew then that broken mess was the person whom he truly loved.

Phillip's grace toward me showed me what God's grace was like. Phillip's love for me showed me how God loves me. His example taught me that I didn't have to earn God's love by doing anything. I just needed to accept it. So, I did. It took time to adjust, but I did.

Our problems were not resolved overnight, but it was a breakthrough. As we worked to overcome my demons together, Phillip never gave up on me. He stayed by my side through it all. He could have decided I was not worth the trouble, but he didn't. Jesus didn't give up on me either and I know now that He never will.

I received God's love and healing grace. I grew to trust both Phillip and God over time as Phillip and I both continued to seek God for His help and healing. In time, we were healed together; me from the effects of my abuse, and Phillip from the effects of the effects of my abuse. Through it all, we both loved each other and had grace with each other. This experience was an example of, and testament to, the boundless love and grace that God has for us.

My story is one that shows that true grace and love are not predicated on our performance or having to earn it. My experience has not only shown me God's kind of love, but it also healed a deep wound that saved my marriage – and my life.

You may not have a Phil in your life to exemplify God's love for you, but I am your Phil, telling you right now that you are worthy of love outside of what you do. God's arms are wrapped around you tightly, protecting, and comforting you, not because you perform well, but because you are precious to Him.

You might be wondering why I would share such a private matter in my public book. I do so because I want you to know my story. There are lessons to be learned from it, and remember, I am authentically Laurel now, so I don't mind sharing myself with you. What lessons can we learn from my story?

First, (and this really goes without saying) don't ever abuse a child. Period. If you find you are tempted to abuse children in any way, please find help now. Really, put the book down and go find help. Call a therapist, talk to your pastor, or both.

Second, if you have been abused, seek help and loving support, and know that you are loved by God. His healing hands hold you now; trust Him. Never forget that. You might need to find professional help as well. Don't be ashamed of that, but realize you are worth the care.

And third, radical grace is real. The message about

radical grace is relevant whether or not you have endured abuse. You do not need to work or do good things to receive God's love.

As I have mentioned, our society is a work-for-reward system. I'm not necessarily against this system in certain circumstances, but the problem is that we replicate that work-reward system in areas where it is damaging, such as our relationships with our children, spouses, and God. Work hard, do good, obey, serve well, and you will get rewarded, appreciated, and loved.

We are told we must do good deeds, so we don't disappoint God. We end up falling right into the trap of thinking that God's love, and therefore His grace, are based on our obedience to that work.

Oh, my precious friend, this breaks my heart because you don't have to earn God's love or anyone else's. You are worthy of love simply because you exist.

The fact is, you have intrinsic value, and He loves you for who you are, not what you do. Over the years I realized that if God could have grace with me and loves me so much that He died for me apart from my performance, maybe I could love myself and give myself grace as well.

I believe that when we fully embrace the grace and freedom that He afforded us through Jesus and live our lives in full confidence that He loves us intrinsically, that makes Him happy. That makes Him know it was all worth it.

God doesn't do the work-for-reward system. He does the "God so loved the world that He gave His only begotten Son" system (John 3:16). No work is needed for the reward He has already given you!

So, love is not love if it is offered as a response to works or good deeds. That said, we know what love is *not*, but what is it? What *is* love? Jesus exemplifies love for us.

True love serves others. Jesus wants everyone to be saved. That is the whole point of His coming. Jesus wanted to make sure there was a way for everyone to be with Him. So, even though people are sinful and un-righteous, He went to the cross for us. His love was demonstrated to us when He came to die for His brothers and sisters. His purpose in coming was to serve all of humanity in love.

God's love is apparent in what Jesus has done for us. His love drove Him to suffer through the birth, life, and death He experienced when He came to live with us. His love cannot be comprehended entirely, but we can begin to understand His great love for us as we gain a clearer understanding of His Gospel of Grace.

Love is desiring to be with each other. God wants to be with you because He loves you. God created you as a unique treasure to enjoy fellowship with Him. His desire is to have a relationship with you both now and for eternity. It is all about love to Him because He is the very essence of love! The apostle John tells us plainly that God is love in one of his books of the Bible.

And finally, true love does not condemn. Jesus didn't come to condemn you because of your sin. If you feel condemned as a believer in Christ, you have been taught something other than the Gospel of Grace. If you carefully read the four gospels in the Bible, you will see the only people Jesus gets upset with are the legalistic Pharisees. This is because they insisted on believing their righteousness was good enough through their obedience to the law. They rejected Jesus, and His free offer of righteousness through faith in Him. They denied His grace. They refused His love. Jesus came to remove condemnation from our lives, including death itself, and the condemnation of guilt and shame over our past and present failures. He came to love us without any expectations of performance. That is radical grace.

God, who is love, created you special in His love, for the purpose of love and with a loving plan for your life. You are not only loved by God, but you are liked by Him too! He digs you. You are His poem, His masterpiece, whom He created specifically with the gifts and talents He wanted you to have and share. And I'll bet He enjoys watching the smiles on the faces of those with whom you share yourself!

Hearing my story is tough, I know. You may not have had the same type of emotional trauma as me, but even if you haven't experienced abuse, I'm sure you have had doubts about your worthiness of love. That is a wide-spread consequence of being human in a difficult world. I'm telling you though, you are worthy of God's love just because you are His creation.

In the meantime, remember, God loves you no matter what you do or don't do. You don't have to do anything for Him to make Him love you. That's crazy love. That's radical grace.

CHAPTER 10

The Separation Lie

Grace keeps you close.

"Your sin is separating you from God."

"God won't answer your prayers if you are continuing in sin."

"If you willfully sin after you are saved, then you break fellowship with God."

Have you heard claims like these? I have, too many times. I am deeply saddened by statements like these that live on in the Christian community. Separation from God due to our sin is a lie and it is the lie that is doing the separating, not our sin. Once we are in Christ, our sin does not and cannot separate us from God.

My friend, it is so tragic that this lie is driving people away from God because they know they are sinners, and they struggle with guilt about their sin, so when they are told that their sin is causing them to distance themselves from God, they can't help but to get discouraged and give up. That is a hopeless load to bear, and a confusing one too.

Now, I am a very logical thinker. The first time I heard this message taught, I thought of some perplexing questions which led me to seek the answers.

After I sin, am I separated from God for a certain amount of time? If so, how much time?

What do I need to do to get back into His presence? Do I need to do some sort of good deed to counterbalance my sin to gain His fellowship back? (The CODE)

Where is Jesus in that statement? Didn't Jesus pay for my sins? If that's so, why does my sin separate me from Him when the Bible tells me that I am "in Christ"?

Rest assured: if you are in Christ, you cannot be separated from Him. This teaching is a part of the prolific Bootstrap Gospel (see the chapter titled *The Bootstrap Gospel*) we hear today, and it is false. Granted, unbelievers *are* separated from God (spiritually and relationally) by their sin. That is why they need to put their faith in Jesus and His righteousness. But believers who have accepted Jesus as their Savior? We are not and *cannot* be separated from God by our sin.

Why is it important to know this truth?

This teaching is wreaking havoc on people's relationship with God. I have heard so many believers say that because of their sin, bad choices, or wrongdoings, God is not listening to their prayers anymore, God is far from them, or they don't feel the presence of God in their lives. This thinking is fueled by the kind of teaching I am addressing here. Imagine what kind of thought process might develop from this erroneous teaching:

If my sin keeps me from having a relationship with God, He doesn't hear my prayers, and I have driven a wedge between us. And since I can't seem to quit sinning, what hope do I have to ever have a relationship with God? If I ruin that relation-

ship, why should I bother acting as if I do have it? I guess I am just doomed. I can't be a Christian. I'm too broken, too dirty, too sinful. God can't love me. God doesn't love me. I have distanced myself from Him and I can't do enough to make Him happy so I can't be close to Him.

And then those who experience these doubts walk away from Jesus entirely.

To reveal the truth about our relationship with God, I will show you that our sin does not and cannot separate us from Him if we have put our faith in Jesus' righteousness.

I don't know about you, but I like to corroborate spiritual teachings with relevant scripture. The concept that sin separates people from God is addressed in the Old Testament, namely, in Isaiah 59:2.

> *But your iniquities have separated you from your God;*
> *And your sins have hidden His face from you, so that*
> *He will not hear. (Isa 59:2)*

I have often heard this verse cited out of context to justify this legalistic thinking. Let's put it back into context.

I suggest you pick up your Bible and read the entire chapter of Isaiah 59, but I will highlight a couple verses for you to support my point. This chapter starts out in verse one stating that God *can* save and hear people.

Then, as we see in verse two it says that people's iniquities are what separates them from Him and that He won't hear their prayers. Then the bulk of the middle of the chapter lists all the iniquities, or sinful doings, of the people it is referring to.

But verse eleven gives us insight as to *who* the LORD is talking to:

> *We look for justice, but there is none;*
> *For salvation, but it is far from us.* (Isa 59:11)

First, this is written to Israelites who were participants in the Old Covenant, not the New Covenant. Also note, these people are not saved, as mentioned in the second line above. This passage is not talking to you, the New Covenant believer who has put your faith in Jesus Christ. The recipients of this message are people who do not yet have salvation.

Now consider verse 20:

> *The Redeemer will come to Zion*
> *And to those who turn from transgression in Jacob,*
> *Says the LORD.* (Isa 59:20)

Isaiah gives the remedy for this separation. A Redeemer. Jesus! He redeems those who turn to Him. Hallelujah!

If someone uses Isaiah 59:2 to tell you that your sin separates you from God, you can counter with Isaiah 59:20 and say that it *did* separate you *until the Redeemer, Jesus, came and you put your faith in Him*. It took Jesus dying to put an end to the Old Covenant and the separation between God and humanity.

This fact demonstrates why the New Covenant is such good news and why it is a better covenant. In the Old Covenant, people were separated from God because of their sin. They couldn't go past the veil in the temple and into His presence because of their unrighteousness. Likewise, those who choose to remain outside of the promise of Jesus are also separated from God because of their unrighteousness. This is the whole point of Jesus and the New Covenant. He came to bring us near to God, past the veil, and into God's presence by His sacrifice.

Let's explore further. Is there any place in the New Testament that says our sin separates us from God if we live by faith in Jesus' righteousness?

Nope. In fact, it says the opposite.

In Ephesians chapter two, Paul tells us that when we were without Jesus, we had no hope and were without God. He goes on to say that as believers in Christ though, we have been brought near to God because of Jesus' death on the cross. *Brought near!* I love that our God and His grace draws us near to Him and keeps us close.

And don't forget the verse in the Book of Romans chapter 8 that tells us nothing can separate us from God's love.

For I am persuaded that neither death nor life, nor angels nor principalities nor powers, nor things present nor things to come, nor height nor depth, nor any other created thing, shall be able to separate us from the love of God which is in Christ Jesus our Lord. (Rom 8:38-39)

Nothing includes you. Your sin cannot separate you. This is very good news! We can stand firmly grounded in faith that God will not leave us because of our sin, and we cannot separate ourselves from Him because of it either.

Finally, the Bible teaches us the Spirit dwells in those who have faith in Jesus. The Spirit is God. The Spirit has fellowship with us 24/7, while we do righteous things in the Spirit, but also while we do unrighteous things in our flesh. He doesn't un-indwell us every time we do something in our flesh. No broken fellowship.

So, do you wonder if there is any New Testament scripture that tells us we can be separated from God? I looked. There is one verse that says we can be estranged (or separated) from Christ, and how that can happen.

You have become estranged from Christ, you who attempt to be justified by the law; you have fallen from grace. (Gal 5:4)

In other words, if believers place themselves back under the law that Christ freed us from to try to obtain righteousness, they are, in a sense like the Pharisees, rejecting Jesus and His righteousness, and therefore separating themselves from Him. Our works, no matter how good they are, cannot atone for our sins and make us innocent. Only Jesus' blood can do that. Being in

God's grace is what cements our relationship with Him. If we attempt to become righteous through our works, by striving to fulfill the Old Covenant law, or obeying the CODE, we are deviating from the very grace that saved us to begin with. Jesus is our justification, and He justifies (makes righteous) us freely because of His grace.

Hence, ironically, legalism, contrary to being a path to righteousness, is in reality, what separates us from God. If we think we can obtain our own righteousness through what we do, then we are not fully receiving Jesus' sacrifice and gift of being born again.

Put another way, if you believe that your sin separates you from God, it means you believe your sin is more powerful than Christ's blood. It simply isn't true. Otherwise, why did Jesus die on the cross? What was the use?

God is not sitting up in heaven looking down on you waiting to push you away the second you do something sinful. He's not some malevolent antagonist ready to pounce on you, condemn you, and banish you from Him even for a moment. Jesus' mission was and is to draw you to Him and to keep you close. His love for you is evident in His actions. Rest in Jesus and His finished work on the cross. Allow His radical grace to draw you in and to keep you close always.

CHAPTER 11

The Duality

Grace makes us new.

I have been blessed to have participated in several theatrical plays over the years. I thought it was fun to put on a different personality and pretend like I was someone else for a while. I was Bashful in the play, *Snow White and the Seven Dwarfs*, when I was about five years old. That part fit me well which is why my mom requested that dwarf for me. It was nice to pretend that being bashful was okay instead of something I should be ashamed of. My typical behavior was expected while I had on that silly hat.

I never liked myself so pretending to be someone else was great. For a time, I could forget the part of me that I didn't like. Even when I wasn't in a play, I tried to put on a show for the people around me. As I have already explained, I was the good child and student that performed for everyone every day. I hid the angry and destructive me from others. Well, most of the time, anyway. I felt like the Hollywood portrayal of good and evil with the devil on one shoulder and an angel on the other. One moment I was doing great, behaving as I should, and the next I was wanting to punch someone's face. Yep. That's me, Bashful moonlighting as a boxer. Just being authentic here.

I felt so confused!

Later, my therapist told me I should "seek a higher power." So, I sought. During the early years of building my relationship with Jesus and learning about Him I was a sponge. I started reading my Bible and listening to sermons. I went to church and actually paid attention.

But going to church made matters worse. I was told that now that I was a Christian, I should stop sinning. I shouldn't be angry, impatient, or allow myself to be out of control. The Fruit of the Spirit became a nagging list on my fridge that wagged its finger at me every time I passed by. I was taught that I needed to work on being more righteous, more holy, and a better Christian. I needed to clean myself up if I wanted to call myself a Christian. I needed to live by the CODE.

In response, I learned that in all outward appearances I was good at being good. I restrained myself from doing things too terrible. I managed to accomplish the Ten Commandments...mostly. I never stole anything, killed anyone, or worshipped idols. The little angel on my shoulder was doing pretty well to influence me, so everyone thought! But I was miserable. Inside I was judgmental, prideful, angry, and self-righteous. Sounds like sinful stuff to me. I tried to stop being that other person, but I couldn't do it!

The faux Christian message that defined me by my sinful nature kept me from the truth and keeps others from it too. Because of this popular message, unfortunately, many people are experiencing a crisis of faith or even leaving the church entirely. We often feel like we cannot be good enough to be a Christian. The more we try to stop being "bad," the more we start believing we *are* "bad" because of our failure to "be good."

The reason we might have this struggle is because we are puzzled by our dual nature. On the one hand, we learn we are a new creation in Christ, but on the other hand, we find ourselves broken and drawn to sin. It just doesn't make sense. We ask ourselves, *"Which is it? Am I a new creation, or am I broken?"*

The answer is not one or the other; it is both. That is the *only* way to resolve that contradiction. In Christ, we have been born *again*. The first time we were born, it was in the flesh, by way of our mothers, into this world and into our sinful nature. However, in Christ, we are born a second time by the Spirit into God's spiritual kingdom and into our new godly nature. Since we are not yet rid of our fleshly sinful nature, we now have a two-part nature, our sinful old self, and our new spiritual self. That new you is who you *really* are!

Once I understood this concept, I realized that old yucky flesh I was born into was going to be around until I leave it behind when I jet off to eternity. But I also learned that I had a new me that was born into the Spirit, and it is the one that desires to do good and make people happy, not as a man-pleaser, but as someone who esteems others higher than myself; as someone who cares for and loves others. I just have a decision to make; in any given moment, would I allow my flesh to lead, or would I let the Spirit lead?

Understanding our dual nature rectifies the confusion around being made new while still sinning. And because we understand God gave us our new man or woman so we could live in him or her, it helps us to truly get God's grace. The more we get grace, the more we accept ourselves for who we are and trust that God does too. We still possess a fleshly nature, but we are born anew into a spiritual existence. We have two natures, but once we are born again, who we *are* is the spiritual one. The real us, the true us, our spirit and soul, are, for a time, dwelling in these bodies in the earthly kingdom and we share space with our sinful nature. But our real citizenship is in the kingdom of God, which is spiritual and eternal. Until we get to our real home, we must deal with this fleshly body and the sinful nature that resides in it. The beautiful news is that we have been born into something incredible by the Spirit.

Let's explore our two-part self a little. As you know, the word *flesh* has a dual meaning. It means our earthly human body of skin, organs, and bones. It also means our temporal, human nature which is drawn to sin and runs contrary to God. Paul calls our sinful nature of flesh the *old man*.

We will not, and cannot, take either version of our

flesh with us into eternity. God will have to transform our bodies before we get there.

Our skin and bones can be corrupted. Our bodies get sick, shut down, feel pain, and deteriorate. We grow old, and eventually, these bodies give up and die, and we leave them behind. Likewise, our sinful fleshly nature is also corrupted. That part of us is selfish, jealous, ungracious, unloving, and desires to pull us toward destruction every chance it gets. But we get to leave that part of us behind too! Praise God we get to leave our earthly bodies and sinful nature behind when we step into eternity!

Good thing, because our flesh can do no good. In fact, Paul tells us that it grows corrupt. It keeps getting worse! It gets worse as it lusts after sin. If our sinful nature grows more corrupt, why do we think that we can force it to get better through our own efforts? The Bible also tells us that it profits us nothing and we should have no confidence in it!

Since these things are true, it is useless to try to obey the law or fulfill the CODE to be a better Christian. We cannot do it. We cannot approach a spiritual life in our flesh. When we do, we are trying to do the impossible.

Our flesh is weak in the face of temptation. It is unrighteous, unclean, imperfect, corrupt, and cannot inherit the kingdom of God. It is unspiritual. It offers no benefit to us, and we should never put our trust in it. We cannot rely on striving in our flesh to make our flesh better. All the effort we can muster in our own strength will not keep our flesh at bay. Making rules for ourselves doesn't make our flesh able to obey or become better; it just frustrates us that our efforts are useless.

Our flesh is what drives us into temptation. Our old man or woman is responsible for all the unrighteous things we do. I'm not saying this as if we shouldn't take responsibility for our actions. That is not at all my point. However, my point is that if we can see our flesh for what it is, then we can choose to stop giving our flesh control of our lives.

How do we do that? Through the power that the Spirit gives us to do just that in our newly created spiritual self, our new man or woman. The Spirit produces the fruit of self-control. Think of it as "flesh-control."

Through our new spiritual birth, we have been given a spiritual nature that is best friends with the Spirit living in us. Paul calls it our *new man.*

When we are born again, we are made new! Our spirit is revived. We are baptized by the Spirit.

You have read the verse in 2 Corinthians, I'm sure. We are a new creation in Jesus. Paul wanted his readers to know that *all things have become new.* We need to realize our old self, while he or she hangs around for a while longer, is not a part of our new nature. Our new nature is something else entirely. And because of the Spirit of God living in us, our natures are not equal and opposite.

The prophet Ezekiel gives us insight into this a bit. He writes that the LORD says He will provide us with a new heart and spirit. Then He says He will give us the Holy Spirit to dwell within us.

Our spirit is made alive and is separate from our sinful flesh. This is our new part. And our new man or woman has been imputed the very righteousness of Jesus because of our faith in His righteousness. It is made holy, clean and is totally separate from our old self. Our spirit and the Holy Spirit are best buddies, and they talk to each other. The Spirit guides, comforts, and helps us. When we submit to Him, we are living *in* His righteousness.

Because our two natures are separate, our new nature cannot be tarnished by our old nature and has everything it needs to walk in love and live the life God wants for us. God created the new us, the real us, neither encumbered nor held down by the old us. Paul tells us that we are no longer slaves of sin and that with every temptation, God will give us a way to escape.

Our two natures are at odds with each other all the time. That is why we struggle. Paul gives us a powerful picture of this struggle between our flesh and our spirit in his letter to the people of Rome. In chapter seven, Paul shares with us that he struggles with his flesh. He wants to do one thing but ends up doing something else that he hates doing. Does that sound familiar? It does to me.

Then Paul says something intriguing. He says that it is no longer him that does the thing he hates, but the sin that lives in him. What? It isn't him? He is referring to his old man, not the real person that Paul is and was created to be. He makes the distinction between his flesh and his spirit. Two parts of the same person. He recognizes the depravity of his flesh, and sometimes, even if he wills to do good (his new man), it is hard to do.

Paul concludes the passage with a question: "Who will deliver me from this body of death?" (Romans 7:24)

Notice Paul doesn't ask, "How can *I* get rid of this body of death?" Or "How can I be a better Christian?"

Paul asks, "*Who* will deliver me...." As my hubby always says, "It's not a 'how-to' it's a 'who-to'." This subtle difference is key. This is the difference between you trying to be less sinful in your own earthly strength versus you understanding Jesus already took care of your body of death by giving you a new spirit and separating the two from each other. He gave you every-thing you need to live your life as the new you. In your new nature you have the ability, by the power of the Spirit, to block your fleshly nature from having its way.

Jesus died and rose again to release you from the bondage of that old nature. He baptized you by the Spirit into a new spiritual kingdom, His Kingdom. Then He gave you His righteousness, made you holy, and gave you the Spirit as your co-navigator. He made you into a new man or woman. And that new nature is extraordi-nary. That new part of you is *life* because of righteousness. Grace has made you new! That is radical grace.

Jesus has released you from the control of your old flesh. That old person was crucified with Jesus, the Bible explains. Now, you are free to live your life as the new you. Does that mean you always will? No. Like Paul's struggle, you will struggle too. I do.

For me, just knowing I can walk in the Spirit and no longer have to walk in the flesh, that my old flesh and new spirit are separate, and that my flesh can be denied control, has changed the way I live. I can look at myself and my mistakes more analytically instead of emotionally. With the Spirit's help, I can see when I am allowing my sinful flesh to rule and make a choice to switch and give control to my new godly nature. But more importantly, I can choose the Spirit, because I am alive to Christ, and serve in righteousness in any moment.

You can too.

Furthermore, since your old self is messed up and you can't do anything to make it better, you can stop trying to make him or her better. Just rest. Rest like God said you could. Rest in knowing that who you are now is a wonderful new spiritual you that walks side by side with the Holy Spirit.

Having two natures and being able to choose which one you give authority to in the moment might be a new idea to you. I will address walking according to the Spirit soon. But first, we need to talk about that new you a bit. You need to fully grasp the magnificence of the new you. God's radical grace has made you radically new!

CHAPTER 12

The Blessings

Grace makes us holy and righteous.

My friend, your frustration with yourself ends here and it ends now! Jesus has given you the most beautiful gift you could ever imagine, and you have been carrying that gift box around with you since you put your faith in Him, but it is time to open that baby up. Let's find out what is in that box and start the celebration!

So far, I have carefully walked you through the history and reasoning of how you came to acquire this gift. I have cleared the path of the debris of false doctrine and legalistic teaching so you could dance your way into this chapter and discover the beautiful blessings that are hidden inside that glittery gold-wrapped package of grace.

While most Christians don't deny that they have that box in their backpack, they haven't opened it up, so they aren't quite sure of its contents, and they are missing the blessing of enjoying what's inside. Not fully understanding the beauty of the gift of God is how we get 34% of Americans, who admit they are sinners, still claiming *they* are working to rectify their sin. The good news is that 28% rely on Jesus to overcome their sin. They must have peeked inside. The other 38% either are fine with being a sinner, don't believe they sin, or prefer not to say.[5]

What happened with that 34%? That is a shocking number to me. A third of Americans are unaware that they can't make themselves righteous by trying not to sin, because they can't escape their sinful nature while still on planet earth. None of us can become less of a sinner in our flesh. God has made it clear that we were born into unrighteousness, and we can't do good things to make us more righteous. Righteousness is not measured on a scale or by a percentage. You are either perfectly righteous, or you are not righteous at all. It is on or off, and remember, we are all born into sin, so we are born in the off position by default. We can never perfect our own righteousness no matter how hard we try.

Now, I am not condoning sin here. I am willing to bet, as a child of God, you really don't like your fleshly sin. That's one reason why you came to Jesus, right? You are a child of God; you know what is right and wrong. God wrote that into your heart and mind. But I am telling you that our flesh doesn't need the boundless freedom of God's radical grace to motivate it to sin. We all sinned before we had mercy and grace, and we will sin in His mercy and grace. That's why it's called mercy and grace. We can't change our flesh, but it can be dealt with differently thanks to Jesus.

In Christ, our spirit has changed. Our new clean spirit

hangs out with God's Spirit 24/7. The Spirit is like our big brother who wants to show us the ropes. As we look to Him to show us how to walk according to Him, He answers. And as we live in His guidance, we will notice we are a part of a higher calling than working on our sin. That higher calling is to love. When we love, sin is the farthest from our minds, and we deny our flesh access.

We can do this because *He* made us righteous and holy and gave us His Spirit to live with us. That's what is in our gift box! We are justified and sanctified by Him. These are spectacular gifts!

When Jesus came to earth to bless every nation, as the covenant with Abraham promised, He went well beyond the gift of eternal life. According to the book of Ephesians, Jesus has given us every spiritual blessing in Christ. We have access to every spiritual blessing! Wow! I don't even know what all of those are, but I discover more and more of them each day I live in Christ.

Let's talk about a few of those blessings. Words like *justification, sanctification, righteousness,* and *holiness* sound good, but what do they mean? I have heard people call these types of words *Christianese*; big fancy words that come from the Bible. Once I understood their definitions, the gospel became so much brighter to me, and more importantly, grace became clearer to me, which helped to free me from the bondage of legalism and the faux gospel

I had been taught.

Justification and *righteousness* are related to each other. They have the same root word which means *right, just, free from guilt*, or *innocent*. The main difference between these two words is that justification is the status of being *declared* innocent and righteousness is the quality of *being* innocent.

For example, a criminal defendant who is acquitted of a crime in a court of law is justified or *declared* innocent, whether they did the crime or not. Furthermore, a person who did not commit the crime *is* innocent and free from guilt. Jesus is this person. He *is* righteous. He is perfectly just, sinless, and innocent. However, we are born into sin, and therefore guilty, but He separated us from that old person and has *declared* our new person innocent and free from guilt. He acquits us. Then, He imputes His righteousness to us, and we are *made* innocent in our new spiritual nature. We are both declared righteous and made righteous because of our faith in the Lord Jesus.

With that foundational truth in place, let's look at what the Bible tells us about our justification and righteousness. The Bible makes it clear that we are not and cannot be made righteous or be justified by being obedient or trying to obey the law. The law only shows us that we are unrighteous and that we need a Savior, as I have already discussed.

But now, through faith in Jesus, we are declared innocent and made righteous. The faithful are *made* righteous! Jesus justifies the guilty who put their faith in Him, and He assigns His righteousness to them.

Your spirit is made righteous, not your flesh. Remember, your flesh grows corrupt and cannot do anything good on its own. But your new spiritual nature is not tainted by sin. It is innocent. It is guilt-free. It is righteous.

Remember the verse in Second Timothy that tells us that we are instructed *in* righteousness. We need instruction on our new life in righteousness, not on how to become righteous. Jesus not only gave us the *ability* to do good things, but His word trains us and equips us to do them.

Your identity is righteousness; you just need training in that righteousness. For example, when someone enlists as a Marine, they *are* a Marine, they just need training in *being* a Marine.

Two other words have a similar relationship. *Sanctification* and *holiness* share the same root word that means *holy, pure, clean, consecrated,* or *separated to God.*

The difference between these two words is that *sanctify* is a verb that means to *make holy,* and *holy* is the adjective that describes a person or object that *has been sanctified.* You have been sanctified, and because of that you are holy. For example, when I walked down the aisle at my wedding, my last name was my father's surname, but the moment I said, "I do" my name changed to my husband's surname. Marriage is the event that made me an Appel. Sanctification is the event that made me holy. I received both my new name and my holiness in an instant. Jesus sanctified me the moment I received Him as my Lord.

When you accept Jesus' sacrifice for your own, you are born again and are separated from the old you and the new you is delivered into His spiritual kingdom. I don't even begin to understand how God performs this miracle, but the Spirit sanctifies you when you are born again and because you have been sanctified, you are holy. You are not *being* made holy. You are not *being* sanctified. You *have been* sanctified and because of that, you *have been* made holy. You are set apart, or consecrated to God, and cleansed, separately from your flesh.

When Jesus was talking to Peter, just prior to going to the cross, after washing his feet, He told Peter that he was already clean, speaking of his sanctification. And Paul makes the same point to the people of Corinth. He plainly states that they were washed, sanctified, and justified in the Lord Jesus by the Holy Spirit.

Because we who are in Christ are righteous and holy in our new spirit, we live in that unblemished innocence. Our new self already exists in that state, so we may simply use this blessing to saturate our actions and words with love. No matter what we are doing or who we are interacting with, love is the motivation and means by which we interact, and we are living according to the Spirit in righteousness and holiness. We don't have to muster it up, work on becoming, or strive to obtain these blessings, they are already a part of us. What incredible and fantastic news!

The good news of our new righteousness has escaped many people. If we are already made righteous and holy, why are we repeatedly told we need to make ourselves better Christians and work on our sins to make God happy? This is the message that is being heard by those 34% of Americans who are striving to become less sinful, but in doing so are missing the point entirely.

This is what I call the "pull-yourself-up-by-your-bootstraps" gospel, or the Bootstrap Gospel, which I will discuss fully in a coming chapter. It is not the true Gospel of Grace because it leaves out the great news that our spiritual nature is already sanctified and clean. Any message that promotes righteousness or holiness through our own effort to sin less is futile and legalistic. It is a *Jesus plus me* message. And that message is causing damage to the body of Christ.

This false teaching that we need to make ourselves better for God's approval drove one man Phillip and I know to desperation. This man's past was checkered with choices that led to sad consequences. He had been married several times, he had cheated on each of his ex-wives, and he was a habitual drug user. However, he knew Jesus. He just didn't know that the gospel he had been taught was not the Gospel of Radical Grace.

He told Phillip that he felt he must be going to hell when he dies because of all the bad things he has done. He even tried to get Phillip to assure him that the good that he had done for his children was enough for God to forgive him for the rest. Phillip explained to him that he was already forgiven. He simply needed to trust in the righteousness of Jesus. Jesus imputed His righteousness based on that faith but that didn't mean he wasn't still drawn to sin in his flesh. Phillip tried desperately to convince the man that God loved him and that his salvation is by faith alone through God's grace. The man couldn't accept that truth and hung up the phone on Phillip. He had been so influenced by people in the community telling him that his righteousness depended on himself that he just couldn't accept that God loved him that much. Sadly, he died a couple weeks later.

We lament that our friend did not accept that he was already made holy and righteous when he put his faith in Jesus and that he was no longer a slave to his sin, but to righteousness. Jesus had given him the goods to do great things. He simply couldn't believe that was true.

What great things am I talking about? I'm talking about love, manifested in a million different ways. Jesus has equipped us to love others, not only those easy to love, but those we don't really know, and even our enemies. The prophet Ezekiel told us that God would give us a new heart, and He did when we gave ours to Him.

I believe that if you don't think you can love others, it is because you don't yet fully grasp radical grace. That was the case for me. Or you just might not know you have that power inside you already. You might be like a superhero who just discovered the amazing power you didn't know you had. God gives us this beautiful ability to love others, truly love them, from a compassionate and caring heart.

I'm not talking about being a conduit for God's love. I've heard people say, "I'm letting God love them through me." That's not love. Think about being on the receiving end of that statement.

So, you are so put off by me that you can't love me yourself, but you are going to graciously allow God to use you as a conduit for His love?

I don't think God needs us to be a pipe for His love to flow out to others. God tells us to love our neighbors, not to let Him love our neighbors through us. Love is a blessing that emanates from our own hearts toward others. And because our spirit draws its power from the Holy Spirit and is separate from our flesh, we *can* truly love others.

Jesus suffered and sacrificed so you wouldn't have to spend your days focused on your sinful self. He went to the cross so you could focus on the good stuff. You are now able to walk in your new beautiful righteous spirit who has been made pure, is holy, and is set apart to worship God and love people.

My friend, you have everything you need to love others because God so graciously gave it to you. Through faith in Jesus' righteousness, you have been made both righteous and holy. You are clean, you are innocent, you are ready to live free and unashamed. Rip that paper off your box, open it up, and start enjoying the gifts God has given you by His radical grace.

CHAPTER 13

The Sanctification Myth

Grace means we don't have to work.

"Insanity is doing the same thing over and over and expecting different results."[6]

This wisdom resonates with me when it comes to how I think about my life before accepting God's radical grace. For years, I tried to be a better person and did good things to make myself *more holy*, but I never felt like I was getting there. And the fruitlessness, or insanity of that cycle drove me crazy. I couldn't do it. I would think I was making progress, but then I would find myself falling back into the same old pattern of sin. I kept expecting different results each time I yanked on my bootstraps and tried to be a better Christian, but the results didn't change.

The process of gradually becoming more holy is a popular teaching called *progressive sanctification*. I hadn't heard the of the term until later in my Christian walk, but I had been taught the general concept in the early churches I went to. Progressive sanctification basically means that by grace you have been saved for eternity, but in this life, because you are still sinful, you and God must work together to make you more holy, more Christlike, as you deny yourself and work on your sinful attitudes and actions. This kind of "sanctification" is a process whereby you become more like Jesus gradually over time through dedication to the CODE and spiritual discipline.

A telltale sign of progressive sanctification is the use of comparatives, such as *better*, *more*, or *less*. Advocates of this principle suggest that you can become *more* Christlike through doing *better*, doing bad things *less*, or doing *more* of the good stuff, and as you are disciplined to work on yourself, with God's help, of course, you are becoming *more* holy. However, you are reminded that you won't ever get to 100% this side of heaven. That doesn't happen until you walk into eternity. Then, you shed your sinful self and are finally, and completely, sanctified.

Progressive sanctification often focuses on backsliding, which is a term that speaks of losing grip of the forward ground you'd already taken. This teaching emphasizes that if you do backslide, you need to get yourself back up and try again. Never give up. God's got you. Don't quit. And at some point, after all the ups and downs and failed attempts, you think you must be crazy. Or maybe you weren't ever a *real* Christian. That's what many people end up thinking.

Progressive sanctification doesn't make sense given that we are a two-part person. As I have talked about already, you can't make your old man or woman better or more holy and you can't make your new man or woman holier than it already is. The very concept of progressive sanctification runs contrary to the truth of *already being* holy, and that our flesh only grows more corrupt, cannot be made better, and cannot be trusted.

Jesus made you righteous and holy, broke the bondage of your flesh, gave you a new spirit and the Holy Spirit to live in you, and thus created you as a new Christlike person. Simply put, because God's grace is radical, you are already like Jesus, and you have everything you need to love like Jesus.

I know I'm going against the teachings of pretty much every mainstream Christian organization. But I tried doing the gradual holiness method for about twenty years and I didn't see any progress. Now I understand it was because I was trying to do the impossible job of cleaning up my old flesh.

Frustrated with how things were going while riding the sanctification rollercoaster, I embarked on a quest to figure out what the Bible might say about progressive sanctification. Interestingly, the concept is not even in the Bible. Sanctification, yes, but the idea that we are slowly sanctified over our lifetime isn't there. Nowhere. So, where do the teachers of this doctrine get their inspiration? What scripture do they use to justify this doctrine?

There is a verse in Second Corinthians that is incorrectly cited to justify it. We will look at it closely so you can see this scripture for what it really is, in all its beauty and truth.

In Paul's second letter to the church in Corinth he encourages them that they can have hope and not be discouraged in suffering. He explains to them that before coming to Jesus, people's minds are blinded, and their hearts are veiled to the truth of the glory of the New Covenant. However, that blindness is lifted in Christ. He takes away the veil and we are transformed. We can see the glory of the New Covenant, so therefore, we don't need to lose heart when times get tough. Although we are hard-pressed, perplexed, persecuted, and struck down, we are not crushed, in despair, forsaken, nor destroyed. In that context, Paul wrote the following verse.

But we all, with unveiled face, beholding as in a mirror the glory of the Lord, are being transformed into the same image from glory to glory, just as by the Spirit of the Lord. (2 Co 3:18)

Some interpret this verse to mean that we are all being transformed into the image of Christ as we sin less and obey more or follow the CODE. But is that really what Paul is saying?

Looking at what the verse states and the verse's context clarifies Paul's message, so let's examine it carefully.

First, this verse says nothing about obeying the law or some set of rules like the CODE. In fact, it doesn't mention any work on our part at all. It only mentions we are being transformed by the Spirit of the Lord. So, let's assume that obeying the Old Covenant law or obeying the CODE has nothing to do with this verse. That's fair, right?

Second, context is critical here. Paul has just spent the previous eleven verses in this chapter comparing the Old Covenant (the law) to the New Covenant. He makes the case that while the Old Covenant was glorious, the New Covenant is even more so. In fact, he calls the Old Covenant the *ministry of death* and the New Covenant the *ministry of the Spirit* at the beginning of the third chapter.

> But if the ministry of death, written and engraved on stones, was glorious, so that the children of Israel could not look steadily at the face of Moses because of the glory of his countenance, which glory was passing away, how will the ministry of the Spirit not be more glorious? (2 Co 3:7-8)

Paul then adds:

> For if the ministry of condemnation had glory, the ministry of righteousness exceeds much more in glory. (2 Co 3:9)

Note the astounding distinction Paul makes here. He calls the law the ministry of condemnation because the law can only condemn us by pointing out the fact that we are transgressors of it. But much more importantly, he calls the New Covenant a ministry of *righteousness*. And not only that, but it also exceeds in glory compared to the Old Covenant. Please don't miss these astonishing and wonderful truths of the Gospel.

Paul continues:

> For what is passing away was glorious, what remains is much more glorious. (2 Co 3:11)

While the Old Covenant was glorious, the New Covenant is much more glorious. At the end of this section, he writes the verse we are analyzing, verse 18.

Paul argued that those in Christ have passed from one glory, the Old Covenant, or law, to a new glory, Christ, and the New Covenant. So, the faithful have passed from the old glory to the new and better glory, or, from glory to glory.

With that in mind, let's look at another part of the verse in question.

It says, "...*we all, with unveiled face, beholding as in a mirror the glory of the Lord....*"

In other words: we (who are in Christ) with unveiled face (ours is uncovered in Christ so everyone can see our face, including ourselves) beholding (seeing) as in a mirror (as if we were looking into a mirror) the glory of the Lord (the glory of Jesus). When we, who are in Christ, look into a mirror, we see the glory of Jesus. How can we see the glory of Jesus if we are not yet transformed, not yet holy? It is because we *are already* holy that we can see the glory of Jesus in the mirror.

Finally, let's explore the final part of the verse. "...*are being transformed into the same image from glory to glory, just as by the Spirit of the Lord.*"

The point is that followers of Jesus are being transformed, individually but also as a group over time, into a similar glory, or image of Jesus, by turning from the glory of the Old Covenant to the new and better glory of the New Covenant. Our initial decision of faith is when the transformation happens. The Spirit makes people holy and righteous when they receive the Gospel of Grace and become New Covenant believers. We are transformed into the image of Jesus when we accept the New Covenant, or new glory. Grace means we don't have to work to become holy; we simply put our faith in Jesus and receive holiness.

As you can see, it is imperative to keep the context of scripture in mind when interpreting it. If we ignore the first part of this chapter, we miss the meaning of this verse. I used to accept the false interpretation of this verse because I had never taken the time to figure it out on my own. This mishandled explanation sounded *Christiany* but teasing out the meaning seemed like it would fry my brain, and after all, that's what the "experts" said it meant, so I accepted their interpretation. But that was before I learned the definition of insanity.

When a person gives up trying to fulfill the law for their righteousness and receives the righteousness of Jesus through faith in Him and His ministry of righteousness, they have passed from the law, which was glorious, to an exceedingly better glory of the Gospel of Christ. It is then that they are transformed into the likeness of Christ by the Holy Spirit (in their new spiritual self). Once you are in Christ, you reflect His glory in the mirror because He has transformed you.

The progression we see in our lives as followers of Christ is not us becoming more like Jesus. It is the progression of learning to walk in our given holiness and righteousness as we more fully receive God's radical grace and truly believe He has made us new and given us everything we need to live as that new transformed person. When we were born the first time, in the flesh, we had to learn to walk in the physical world. Now that we are born a second time, by the Spirit, we must learn to walk in the spiritual world. Like a young child who goes from crawling, to waddling, to walking, to running, we also slowly but surely advance in our walk in Jesus' grace.

This false interpretation of 2 Corinthians 3:18 has entrapped countless believers in legalistic living, and in doing so, has robbed them of a Biblical understanding of God's grace.

Working on sin is the opposite of grace. We (our new selves) have been separated from our sin (our old selves) and our sin doesn't have control over our new selves. Why, then, does the teaching of progressive sanctification tell us we should spend our time trying to better the corrupted, ugly part of ourselves? If you have ever read Paul's letters, you know he calls this effort *works*. Works are the opposite of grace. Grace means we get to rest from working on our sin. Jesus already forgave us for our sins and removed any power sin had in our lives.

Progressive sanctification requires us to obey the law of Moses, the Ten Commandments, or the CODE to get our sin under control and become more holy. We are told, "Don't do this, do that better, be more this, be less that." Remember, we are not under the law if we are in

Christ and obeying the law cannot make us righteous anyway. We are in the grace of God, not under the law. We are enabled to live in righteousness and walk in love by the power of God's Spirit living in us. There is no rule or law against that.

Teachers of progressive sanctification assert we are not already sanctified. They must teach this because, in their view, if we were holy, we wouldn't sin. Therefore, because none of us is sinless, they conclude that we must not be holy.

There is another explanation that makes more sense: our dual nature. Because of the grace of Jesus, by the Holy Spirit, He has already made us holy, apart from our sinful nature. See, progressive sanctification misses the mark because it doesn't recognize our two natures. Our new spirit nature is holy, and our old fleshly nature is still sinful. In Christ we are both our old part and our new part, which is how it is possible for us to be both tempted to sin and holy at the same time.

Jesus suffered and sacrificed so you wouldn't have to spend your days focused on your sinful nature. He went to the cross so you could focus on the good stuff: the new sanctified part of you. Because Jesus has sanctified us, we can rest in Him. No more working for our holiness. No more insanity.

The arduous, insurmountable struggle to "clean yourself up" in order to become holy is a lie, one that prevents us from living free and unashamed. However, by embracing God's radical grace, we can do just that.

CHAPTER 14

The Walk

Grace lives in us.

I used to encourage my youngest granddaughter to
practice walking.

"Get back up, honey. You can do it!"

"Come on, come to LaLa."

"You can do it, baby girl!"

She had just turned one year old and was trying very
hard to keep up with her older sister. She walked like a
drunken cowboy; bow-legged and wobbly, and she fell
down every few steps.

If you have children, you know what I am talking
about. As sad as it is to see them struggle and fall so
much, it is what they must do to learn, so we encourage
their effort.

This is how I see my walk in the Spirit. I take some
steps, wobble, and fall down, but I have learned to get
back up and step back into God's kingdom and my
spiritual self as soon as I can.

I'm sure you have heard the phrase *walking in the
Spirit* or heard someone talk about how they are *led by the
Spirit*. When I first heard about this concept, it sounded

spiritual, mysterious, and bewildering. I read in Galatians that if we live in the Spirit, we should walk in Him, but that didn't make sense to me until I learned about my two-part nature. Once I realized my mind could choose to give control to my flesh or my new spirit nature, this concept became clear. It made sense, so I tried it out.

I wish I could say I mastered it overnight. I'm still learning, but it comes to me more naturally now than when I first started. Having seen God work in situations where I have submitted myself to His Spirit has developed a stronger faith that walking in the Spirit is our new mission. I see that allowing the Spirit into any situation fosters love, mercy, healing, grace, peace, and reconciliation. I had to begin learning about walking in the Spirit as an adult, but we were blessed to begin teaching our children from the start. I'll share an example of fostering this type of response in our children.

If you are a human being, and I'm guessing you are, you understand sibling arguments (even if you don't have siblings yourself). My kids were very good kids, thankfully, but they did have their moments, like fighting over something that we adults would think is ridiculous. But, in their little world, it was worth going to war over.

One time, when my son was four and my oldest daughter was two, they got into a little fist fight. My daughter hit him because she felt frustrated. She didn't know any better. But for some reason, I don't even know, that day my daughter hit my son in the arm, and he hit her back. Now, my son wasn't crying because his sister's punch in the arm didn't hurt. But my daughter? Oh my, did she scream and wail like she was being tortured.

My mom would have told my brothers and me to stop fighting and crying or she would give us something to cry about. I always thought that approach was counterproductive because I *obviously* already had something to cry about. This frustrated me as a child and made me even madder. Yet when I became a parent, I understood what she was thinking. She got tired of her kids fighting and just wanted us to be quiet. I love my mom, but this was a fleshly approach. It wasn't about love; it was about silence and obedience. And it didn't teach me how to deal with conflict with my brothers.

Phillip and I decided we would raise our children to approach conflict spiritually instead of in a fleshly manner. This situation demanded that I talk to them. I asked them to put themselves in the other's shoes and try to imagine what it feels like. I asked them what they thought the other was feeling and asked them to verbalize it. I also allowed each of them to express their feelings without interruption by the other. Then I sat with them and mediated their conversation until they could honestly and contritely apologize to each other. Even at their young age, they learned that day what loving one another looks like. They understood each other's feelings and honed their compassion. That didn't mean they never fought again, but when they did, I applied the same process. Soon, they no longer needed me to mediate, and they became great friends who still love and respect each other as adults.

We were blessed to have been able to begin this learning process with our children at a young age. I know not everyone has that opportunity, but I fully believe that anyone who desires to teach their children, or learn themselves, about walking in love can start at any moment. They can learn about the spiritual approach to life, not only for conflict, but also to love others as God has loved us.

Walking in the Spirit means that we walk in love. Because Jesus died for us and gave us our new righteous nature, we can step into that person's shoes at any moment in our day. Even if we have been wearing those old man or old woman shoes for a while.

In Paul's letter to the Ephesians, he talks about putting off our old man and putting on our new man. In the middle of these two exhortations, he tells us to *be renewed* in our minds so that we can put on the new man. We need to think a new way. Knowing now that you *can* put off your flesh and live as the new you makes it possible. It is just a decision. Not an easy one sometimes, for sure, but possible.

So, our minds sit between our old fleshly self and our new spiritual self. At any moment we can choose to give either one control. When we choose to deny our flesh control, we are walking in the Spirit because our new self is spiritual and allows the Holy Spirit to lead.

Let's take a moment to understand the Holy Spirit. Because we don't totally understand Him, we tend to avoid learning or talking about Him and we relegate Him to some mysterious being "somewhere out there." However, it is good to realize who He is and what His mission is, which will help us to enrich our relationship with Him.

The Bible tells us quite a bit about the Spirit. He is the Spirit of God. He is one member of the triune God. His mission is to convict the world of sin and testify about Jesus. Then, once we become a child of God, He becomes the guarantee of our salvation, and we are baptized with Him. The Spirit sanctifies and justifies those who put their faith in Jesus.

Jesus told us before He went back to be with the Father that He would send the Helper, the Holy Spirit, to come live inside of us. The Spirit's ministry is to be a part of our daily lives. His mission is to intercede for us with the Father and talk to Him on our behalf. He is our guide as He communes with our spirit. He gives us spiritual gifts and produces godly fruit in us. He comforts and leads us as we walk in Him.

I like to think of the Spirit as my counselor. He sits inside of me 24/7 and offers His direction, wisdom, and advice. It's my job to listen. I don't hear Him audibly when He talks to me, but He is that voice that is connected to my thoughts, my soul, and my spirit. I don't know how it works, I can only tell you that I get ideas and desires toward certain things and if they align with love, grace, and His spiritual fruit, I believe they are Him giving me those ideas and thoughts. And when I listen and do the spiritual righteous stuff that He is putting on my heart, that is what it means to walk according to the Spirit.

How do we know what is spiritual new nature stuff versus what is fleshly old nature stuff in any given situation? A good test is to think about whether a given impulse or thought or emotion is a fruit of the Spirit, or its opposite. Here is a list of actions to help us recognize when we are being led by the Spirit versus being led by the flesh. Are we being…

Loving	or	Hateful
Joyous	or	Miserable
Peaceful	or	Hostile
Patient	or	Short Tempered / Intolerant
Kind	or	Mean
Good	or	Wicked / Evil
Faithful	or	Disloyal / Unreliable
Gentle	or	Brutal
Self-Controlled	or	Unconstrained

This is not a list of dos and don'ts. It's not a list of things you need to try to accomplish or eliminate in your life. If you try to do that you will be frustrated because you will be trying to fix your sin nature. That is a legalistic and fleshly approach to living in your new man or woman. It won't work and it won't help.

As I have addressed previously, your flesh is still with you, and you will continue to tick off boxes on the right-hand column more than you want, but the good news is, when you find yourself on that right side, you now know you are in your flesh. You can choose to step into the left side of the list and start walking according to the Spirit and in your new righteous self for the purpose of walking *in* righteousness, not *for* righteousness. To love, not to obey. As mercy, not sacrifice.

I had been taught that the fruit of the Spirit was something I was to pray for. For example, when I was being impatient, I was to pray for more patience. That didn't ever do it for me. I was continually having to go back to this prayer, after feeling guilty for not being good enough. What I didn't realize though, is that I was asking God to do something He had already done. I just didn't know it was available, so I wasn't using it. Now I understand that the Spirit is living in me, and *He* produces the fruit. I can't muster it up in my own strength. He has already provided it for me to apply to my life and it is available to me at any given moment. I just need to take ahold of it and share it. In love, I can do just that because grace lives in me.

I will give you specifics on how this process plays out, practically, in the next chapter.

The Bible tells us that when we are walking in the Spirit, it is impossible for us to be in our flesh. If you picture your mind sitting between your fleshly and spiritual natures, when you choose to walk in one, you can't be walking in the other. If we focus on the good stuff, we won't be distracted by the bad stuff. When our focus is love, and we are allowing our spirit to have control, we are subduing our flesh. And vice versa. When our attention is on our flesh, we are allowing our old man or woman to have control, and we are disregarding our new man or woman. Our outward actions and new inner spirit can be worlds apart when we let our flesh have control. When we walk in love toward others, we are walking and living our lives according to the Spirit and are aligning our outer actions with our inner spirit.

When we are submitted to the Spirit and are being loving, we will not be hating. When we are serving, we can't be selfish. If we are being compassionate, we won't be judging others. If we are walking according to the Spirit, we can't in that exact moment, be walking according to our flesh.

But not hating, being selfish, or judging is not the point of our new lives. Loving, serving, having compassion and grace is the point. Much more critical than not sinning is walking in Christ which produces life and love. Not that our failures don't have consequences. They do. That is why we all desire not to fail. We hate hurting others and don't like feeling shameful about our sins.

But walking in the Spirit is about creating life and infusing love in the lives of those who we encounter each day. These are the things that develop good and lasting connections with people, peace in our households, and forgiveness in our relationships. These are the things that will last for eternity, and walking in love glorifies Jesus, which draws people to Him.

If you are not used to walking in the Spirit like my sweet baby girl learning to walk for the first time, it is an awkward task. You need to strengthen those unused muscles. As you lean into love and grace more and more, allowing His will in your life's circumstances, you will see you can trust Him. You will grow in your relationship with Him, and you learn that walking in the Spirit is a true blessing.

One final thought. If we are focused on sin, we are so distracted with our flesh that we are not doing the very things that bring life and love to the world around us. If you spend all your time thinking about being a sinner, you give your flesh all the attention. If you deprive your flesh of the attention by setting your mind on Jesus, putting on the Spirit, and walking in the new you, you are not providing your flesh the opportunity to be in charge. Rather, your spirit is in control. Additionally, you are accomplishing the very thing God desires for His children. You are living life as the new you, walking in love because His radical grace lives in you.

CHAPTER 15

The Light Switch

Grace makes it possible.

Does the following situation sound familiar?
You are arguing with someone. Ugly words are being exchanged and your blood is boiling. Then, the phone rings. You can't ignore this call, but you can't reveal to the caller you're in the middle of a heated discussion. What do you do? You switch your attitude immediately and answer in a kind, normal voice, "Hello?"

When we flip our attitude and behavior like this, it involves us jumping out of our fleshly self and into our spiritual self in a flash. Whether it is anger, gossip, mischief, or anything of the like, we can put off our old flesh and put on our new spirit as soon as we want to avoid embarrassment or shame. It is an immediate response. There is no time to decompress and transition out of our flesh; we just switch! It's as straightforward as flipping on a light switch.

So, if it is possible to switch from flesh to Spirit just to avoid embarrassment or to put on a good face for someone, it must also be possible to jump into our righteous self at any moment. We can switch to the Spirit for the purpose of love, mercy, and peace. I call this switching to the Light. And that switch, too, can happen in a flash. It just takes motivation and willingness to make it happen.

The truth is, we hold on firmly to our flesh, so it may not seem so easy to jump out of it. But that is because of *our flesh's will*, not *our spirit's capability*. It *is* possible to stop what we are doing and switch gears.

It is better to never be in our flesh in the first place, of course, but that is not the easiest thing to do since we are dragging around our sinful self and he or she demands attention through obnoxious tantrums night and day. So, if we don't walk according to the Spirit all the time, we need to understand how we can make that instant transition. I believe knowing it is possible is the first step. Understanding that grace makes it possible is how we begin to live a life that is defined by love, peace, and forgiveness.

Desiring to walk in love is the second step. As we look to esteem others higher than ourselves and understand the value of love and grace, we find that we are not only willing to walk according to the Spirit, but also excited to see what God can do in situations in which we invite Him to participate as we shut out our flesh. Grace is a great motivation.

The final step is acting on that desire and making the choice to do so. We submit to the Spirit. We speak in love to others' spirit while we reach into the well of compassion and empathy. We put on love. It is such a joy to watch the countenance of a grocery store associate brighten up when you sow love and encouragement into the few minutes you have with them while they check out your items. The associate you must talk to on the phone when you didn't receive what you ordered is especially surprised if you are loving and kind rather than impatient and frustrated like most of their other calls. And power is removed from those who wish you harm when you respond with love. Nothing can win against love. You can put on love when you know it's possible and have a desire to do so.

I'm guessing you want to know how you switch off your flesh when you are smack dab in the middle of frustration and anger. You know you *can* switch to the Light now and you *desire* to switch to the Light, but how do you do it, especially when you are in the fetters of your flesh? How do you choose to do it? What does that actually look like? I would like to share two scenarios with you to help you to understand the process.

First, like anything you are learning to do, practice helps. If you exercise your switching ability when things are calm, it will feel more natural and familiar to do when things are heated.

For years I struggled with impatience at the check-out lane in the grocery store. I'd say it was because I was tired and war-torn from dealing with three kids in a Wal-

Mart, but that would only be an excuse. True, but an excuse. Inevitably there would be a lady in front of me digging in her Mary Poppins bag for that last penny she needed to pay her bill, or the cashier was daydreaming about working at the DMV and was scanning items at the rate of one per minute. These were my triggers.

As I learned more about switching back out of my flesh and into the Light, I realized I didn't have to be so frustrated at the store. I decided to practice walking with the switch on. Remember, the apostle Paul gave us the answer to this process. He said in Ephesians that we put off the old self, we are renewed in the spirit of our minds, and put on the new self. Put off, change our thinking, put on. I decided to give that a try.

Before entering the store, I prayed and asked the Spirit to help me access His fruit of patience. Every time someone triggered me, I did the 180. Whatever is affecting you, do what is 180 degrees the opposite. The way you can put off impatience is to recognize it, decide to set it aside, change your thinking, then put on patience.

When I stood in the line for the cashier, and started to get impatient, I caught those thoughts. Rather than entertaining them and validating them with the obvious facts that proved why I *should* be impatient, I decided those things didn't matter. I put them off. By the power of the Spirit and His fruit of self-control, I shut off that loudmouth flesh. What mattered was love. It didn't matter why penny lady and slow cashier were doing what they were doing, they were beautiful creations of God. They were people with stories, feelings, hopes, and disappointments, just like me. I changed my thinking. I put on compassion. Once I changed my mind about the situation, patience was easily accessed and applied.

Because I recognized my impatience, knew I could respond differently, and chose to change, I prepared myself beforehand and practiced doing the switch until it came natural to me. I don't know how long it took, but I got to where I was able to go to the store and celebrate all the penny ladies and slow cashiers instead of getting impatient with them.

I applied that practice to all the situations in my life that I recognized as habitual and common. That way I was better prepared for the moments that would tap into my anger and frustration and really get me in my flesh. I embraced the importance of walking according to the Spirit, not just for me to *not* walk according to my flesh, but more importantly for me to walk in love.

We have all experienced having an argument with someone. I'm sure you can recall feeling angry, unheard, and frustrated. If you are like me, sometimes I would be so mad that I could barely control myself and the frustration made me want to bring that boxing dwarf Bashful back to life. But once I learned about switching to the Light, in those moments, the Spirit was good to remind me that I was giving in to my flesh. I knew the drill. Put off, change my thinking, put on. Do the 180.

At first, when I was neck deep in my sinful flesh, that transition seemed like I was facing a twenty-foot steel wall that I could never get over. I want you to under-stand that this process appears to be impossible at first when we are in the heat of the moment. But practice is our friend when we are learning something new, and practicing switching off our flesh and on the Light is no different.

Firefighters respond to house fires. They don't react; they respond. Why is that? Because they are trained not to react to an emergency but to know ahead of time, outside of their emotions and fears, what they will do to respond to the situation and be helpful. They have practiced. Like firefighters preparing for how they will respond to a housefire, you can practice ahead of time how you will respond in those difficult moments. That practice helps you to know that switching to the Light is possible and prepares your spirit with a plan of action. And if you practice, you won't react, but you will respond.

The reality is that I would find myself in the middle of an argument, fuming, but thinking about the fact that I was in my flesh and that I could switch to my spiritual nature with the help of the Holy Spirit. Sometimes I would think *I don't want to love; I don't want to be nice, I'm mad.* But I knew I was in my flesh so I would ask for the Spirit's help. And when I asked, the Spirit would always answer me and give me His strength. I desired to walk according to His will and not my own, and He honored that desire.

See, the action of switching is a decision, or response, we make in our minds and hearts, but once we make it, He is faithful to give us the power to lay down our old man or woman and put on our new one. We *can* set aside our flesh and choose love. Do the 180. Do the opposite of yelling, fuming, not listening or being apathetic. Breathe deep, pause, put on the other person's shoes for perspective, foster compassion for their needs, listen, and speak in love.

One of the keys of learning to respond according to the Spirit is to understand your own triggers that draw you into a fleshly reaction. It is helpful to reflect on these triggers, notice how you react, and figure out a spiritual response that is 180 degrees from the fleshly reaction. I know for me some of my triggers are tiredness, pain, and feeling out of control of a situation. What are yours? Take some time for self-reflection and note those things that make you vulnerable to walking in your old man or woman so you can recognize when you are susceptible to the devil's temptations.

I have given you a couple examples of escaping the darkness as you put off the old you, change your thinking and put on the new you. This is a great first baby step. But as followers of Jesus, ultimately it isn't about finding your way *out of the darkness*, it is about finding *the way of light* in everyday life. These first steps I explained are only the beginning of understanding God's radical grace. As you do the 180 you will learn to trust God that He is present with you and is there to bring His light into your life. So now you can walk. It's time to run!

As Christians, we tend to look at our lives as walking through a minefield trying to avoid getting blown up. Walking according to the Spirit is not like walking through a minefield, it is like running through a field of flowers, full of beauty and life. Jesus told us that if we are in Him, we no longer live in the darkness. God's radical grace means we don't have to live as if we are always battling darkness. Jesus already won that battle!

What if instead of switching to the Light at Wal-Mart or in the middle of an argument, and escaping the darkness, you could live in the light all the time? Jesus tells us that is who we are in Him. If we approach every situation with the intent to discover the way of Light rather than the way out of the darkness, that will change everything. It is a subtle difference to describe, but the effects of that difference cannot be fathomed.

God's creation is not like Star Wars where good and evil are equal and opposite forces. God's force, or Light, is far greater than anything in this world. That is why God told us that He who is in us is greater than he who is in the world. God's force of Light is overwhelmingly more powerful than the darkness of our flesh and when we walk through life as a beacon of that Light, we bring love, life, creativity, restoration, forgiveness, and eternal value with us.

I wish I could give you a roadmap of how this plays out in our everyday lives, but God is laying the road as we go. When we are born of the Spirit, we are like the wind, the Bible tells us. We can't predict how He will direct us, but He will create beauty and life in every situation in which we invite Him to get involved. That is altogether terrifying and exhilarating at the same time because we must trust that God can and will work in our lives, but we also get to see what He does, and that is exciting.

I can't give you a roadmap for your life, but I will provide a couple examples of hypothetical situations to help you see the differences between walking in darkness, avoiding darkness, and finding the way of Light. Let's examine them now.

Sue, who works with John, just got a promotion that he believed he would get.

Flesh: John is jealous, gets angry, and starts trash-talking Sue to co-workers.

Spirit/Avoiding Darkness: John starts to get jealous and angry, flips the switch, and avoids trash-talking Sue to co-workers. He even manages to tell her congratulations.

Spirit/Light Living: John looks for the way of light. He trusts God that He will work all things out for his good and He has a plan for him outside of what happens for others. John sees Sue's hard work, appreciates her talents, is happy for her, takes her to lunch to celebrate her promotion. John touts how good Sue is at her job to his co-workers.

Can John see what God is doing for him in this situation? Probably not, but that is where faith comes in. The Spirit will have His way in this situation and John cleared a path for Him to work in his life by walking in the Light and walking in love. This is the very definition of walking by faith, not by sight.

Here is another a hypothetical story. The roles in this example could easily be reversed, so don't get hung up on my seemingly stereotypical example.

Linda and Dan have been married for three years. He works at an accounting firm, but Linda pays the bills because he doesn't want to look at numbers outside of his job. They are struggling to live paycheck to paycheck. Any extraordinary expense puts them in a difficult situation financially. Linda opens their credit card bill that is close to being maxed out. Dan had charged $400 last month at the local golf and country club dining room. He and some of his co-workers would meet each month in the summer to play golf and get lunch together. Someone else usually pays, but last month, Dan offered to pay and put the charge on his credit card.

Flesh: Linda gets angry because she is worried about how she is going to pay the bill. She confronts Dan and chews him out for spending money they didn't have.

Spirit/Avoiding Darkness: Linda takes her angry thoughts captive and flips the switch. She approaches Dan with a loving, non-judgmental tone, and says they need to discuss this charge. She explains to him that they don't have the money to pay for everyone's lunch at the country club. She suggests he stop going and he agrees because he doesn't want to argue, and this seems like a reasonable solution.

Spirit/Light Living: Linda looks for the way of Light. She considers the root issue that drove Dan to pay, rather than address the symptom, which is the charge on the credit card. Her desire is to be on the same team, supporting Dan, rather than being in opposition to him. She imagines why Dan would charge this meal when he knows they didn't have the money. She keeps asking "why" until she gets to the root of the issue. Let's look at her thought process in this hypothetical situation.

Why would Dan offer to pay for everyone's lunch knowing full well he couldn't afford it? Usually someone else pays. He wanted to be the one to pay this time. But why?

Why would he want to pay this time? He probably feels inadequate around his buddies because they don't seem to be struggling with money. Dan's pride caused him to pay. But why?

Why would he risk the argument with me for his pride? He has been struggling with feeling inadequate in other areas of his life lately. He works very hard, puts in a great deal of overtime, very rarely gets to do things for himself, and he is underappreciated for all his hard work at the firm. He probably just wanted to be the hero, the good guy, the one who wasn't needy for once and appear as if he had it all together. But why?

Why was he desperate to be seen as having it together? He has been teetering on the edge of depression lately and feeling like he can't do anything right. He feels ashamed that he doesn't make enough money and that he hasn't climbed the corporate ladder like his buddies have. Enjoying a guy's day out and ignoring the circumstances of his life probably helped him get through the week. The risk of disappointing me was worth the reward, so the reward must have been important to him.

Linda could see that Dan needed her understanding and compassion instead of her judgment and anger. She lovingly asked Dan if her assumptions about his motives and feelings were correct. He was pleased that she knew him so well. She told him she wanted to support him and that she wanted him to go out and have some fun sometimes, but that they needed to work together to prepare for such times. They discussed other items they could cut from their budget so he could have his time with the guys.

Linda also talked with Dan about his feelings of inadequacy and feeling underappreciated. She reassured him that she didn't view him that way. Because she respected him and approached him in love and as an equal partner, she demonstrated her respect for him. They were able to talk through the issues Dan was dealing with at work as well. They walked according to the Spirit as a team rather than against each other while in their flesh.

How do you think Dan would have felt if she had responded in her flesh? He knew he was guilty of spending money they didn't have. He would probably have become defensive and argumentative to protect himself against Linda's attack.

What about if Linda simply approached him, lovingly, about not spending money they didn't have? That may have stopped the financial bleeding, but it would not have addressed the underlying issue that caused Dan to overspend in the first place.

For Linda to take the time to think through the issue, at a deeper level, she demonstrated her love and respect for Dan. He felt understood and valued. This scenario is why I say Spirit living creates life, peace, reconciliation, and eternal value. Linda found the way of Light in this situation which brought her and Dan together rather than pushing them apart. Radical grace made it possible.

The Bible tells us that now that we are born again, our Light switch is in the on position by default. When we recognize we are in our flesh, we can go through the process of putting off, changing our thinking, and putting on for a given situation, but we can also apply that verse in a broader sense as a more permanent exchange.

Walking in the Spirit doesn't feel natural at first because while we are familiar with walking in the flesh that we were born in, walking in the Spirit is entirely new. But in time, we will get more familiar with walking in Him as we wake up each day knowing our new normal is Light and it is our old flesh that is trying to pull us back into the darkness. But we *can* shut him or her down by the power of the Spirit because He is always there to help us to do so.

In each moment you find your flesh rearing up, the Spirit is there to remind you that you don't have to give it control. But if you do, you can switch right back to your spirit. It really is like a light switch. Once you recognize you are in your flesh, you can think about a spiritual response to what is going on, which allows you to direct your focus to put off your old self and put on the new.

But better yet, recognize that you can live with your switch already and always on. When you switch to a spiritual focus, trust God and have faith in Him that He has your best interest at heart and will respond. That doesn't mean the heavens will open up as rainbows and butterflies descend and an orchestra starts playing Pachelbel's Canon in D or that everything bad in your life, including your flesh, will disappear. But it does mean you have invited God into your life for His help, guidance, and blessing. And that, my friend, is walking with God.

I encourage you to walk in the Light along with the Spirit. Put off that old man or woman, put on the new, and answer His call, "Hello?" Radical grace makes it possible.

The Law of Love

Grace is love in action.

"Love is the only force capable of transforming an enemy into a friend."

I appreciate that Martin Luther King, Jr. called love a force. Think about it. God is the force of all creation, and He is love.

Love is the one thing everyone on this planet wants. Sure, some people might say they would rather have money or power, but I propose that even they want to be loved, above all. We create songs, poems, and movies about it, and we seek love from our family, friends, and pets. The need to be loved is a powerful force in our lives.

In the last two chapters, I talked about walking in the Spirit. Walking according to the Spirit brings life, peace, grace, and forgiveness into our lives and relationships. This way of approaching others can even make an enemy a friend. There is an easy indicator that reveals if we are walking in the Spirit or not, and that indicator is love.

The Bible gives us insight into the new law of God, which is to love one another. We are not under the law of

Moses and are freed from the bondage of sin and death, but, more importantly, we are freed *to* something far greater. This is the thing God has desired from His children since the creation of Adam and Eve. This is what He desired for His chosen nation, the nation of Israel, and this is the only thing we are asked to do by Him now that we are called the children of God. This thing is love.

Jesus told His disciples He was giving them a new commandment now that they were a part of the New Covenant. John was faithful to share this with us in his books. Jesus himself said that His new commandment was that we are to love one another. John explains that this new commandment is really the commandment about love found in the Old Testament in the Book of Leviticus.

'You shall not take vengeance, nor bear any grudge against the children of your people, but you shall love your neighbor as yourself: I am the LORD.' (Lev 19:18)

It's new because by Jesus' grace, we have been made righteous and holy and have been given a new spirit along with the Holy Spirit, so now we *can* fulfill that command.

In Romans chapter 13 verse 9, Paul summarizes all of God's commands into that verse from Leviticus, "You shall love your neighbor as yourself." Love is all we are asked to do as New Covenant believers. Everything we do according to the Spirit is a subset of the grand goal of love. Love encompasses all things spiritual and righteous. Do you want to know what to do in any given situation? Love.

So, what does it look like to love others according to the Spirit?

God's love is gracious. His love doesn't impose conditions or expectations. His love for us is pure and all encompassing.

When I think about defining my love for God, I would say I love Him for who He is, and because of who He is, He has done great things for me. Even when He doesn't answer my prayers exactly how I have requested, I still think He is worthy of my worship. I don't walk away from Him if He doesn't do what I ask. Why is that? I guess it is because I know He loves me, has sacrificed for me, and knows what is best for me. But it's not the act of the sacrifice that makes me love Him. I am forever grateful for His sacrifice, but His heart behind the act is what draws me to love Him. I love Him because of His character and heart of love. God's actions might not be *why* we love Him, but they entice us to take note and investigate what kind of God would die to save the world.

Like God demonstrating His love for us through His death on the cross, we too can demonstrate our love for others through the things we do. Love is fashioned in our hearts, but it is demonstrated by our actions. It is walked out by doing things for people, giving our time and resources to others, encouraging, praying, or even forgiving those who have hurt us. Love does for others. Love has compassion for others' plight in life. Love is gracious and merciful.

In 1 Corinthians chapter 13, Paul gives us a definition of love: love is patient, kind, not envious nor rude. It is not selfish, prideful, nor malicious. Love endures everything. When we love others, we are sharing God with them. And when God touches lives, life happens. See, the Bible tells us that the devil's mission is to steal, kill, and destroy. But God does a 180 on the devil, He gives freely, creates life, and restores from destruction. So, when God gets involved, new life, beauty, and reconciliation happens. Love has eternal and spiritual consequences.

It isn't easy to love others. The problem we humans have is we try to love people in our flesh. When we try to love from the view of our flesh, it is hard to look past people's flaws and failures, especially if we have been hurt by them. But God tells us to love them anyway. Jesus told us we can love our enemies, which can sometimes seem like a Herculean task. It is only possible in our spiritual nature by the power of the Spirit and His transformation of our hearts.

I know this to be true. My childhood abuse made me agoraphobic by the time I was twenty years old. I was terrified of people and crowds. I could barely get myself to go to the grocery store. I was not only terrified of people, but I hated almost everyone. After all, they could hurt me, right? So, I protected myself. I stayed home as much as possible. It was my defense mechanism.

But as time went on and I sought the Lord Jesus for answers and healing, I allowed His Spirit to take more and more control of my life. I learned about love and forgiveness and how to look at people with compassion and grace. I could see past their flaws and focus on the beautiful person God made them to be.

That journey wasn't easy. I would wake up every day, stubbornly harboring anger in my sinful nature, but then devotedly praying in my spiritual nature, "Lord, please help me to forgive and to love again." And every time anger and ill will entered my mind, I took my ugly thoughts and placed them in the light of grace. I reminded myself that my offenders' sin, though it hurt me tremendously, was not any worse than mine. This was my daily practice for a decade. Some days, my heart was totally in it. But other days, I forcibly dug my heals into the anger. It was a battle between my flesh and my spirit.

It's okay if your journey to love is slow going or if you are filled with skepticism and unbelief right now. I hear you. If I hadn't been through it, I'd be skeptical too. But I am here to encourage you that learning to love is real. It's radical and real.

Eventually, I learned how to love people again as my heart softened with the help and guidance of the Spirit. I can even say I love the men who abused me. Of course, I don't trust them anymore, but I can have compassion for their struggle and forgiveness for their sin against me. Once I understood how to love in the Spirit, I *had* to love people from my own heart and spirit.

As I submitted to the Spirit, He honored my prayers to love. That's radical grace. And getting to that place of grace helped to heal my brokenness.

But how do we get beyond the hurt?

Walk in love. That is how. We must walk it out after receiving the heart of Christ. We walk in the Spirit, who is love, because God is love, and the Spirit is God. We pay attention to our conscience and that little voice that indicates to us when we are being unloving. Not only do we listen for the Spirit, but we choose to act. He is the one who transforms our hearts, makes them new and pliable. Love is one of the fruits the Holy Spirit produces in His orchard. It is our job to allow our new hearts to beat strong in love. As we recognize that we are in our flesh, we make the decision to switch to the Light, and begin anew, in that moment, with love as the goal. Jesus gave us His Spirit so we *can* love even the most difficult people.

I will share an example with you to show you one of the practical ways I have learned to walk in love. This isn't a very deeply personal example, but it shows you that even in our daily lives we can love other people that we don't even know.

Sometimes I get impatient with other drivers while in traffic. You know the ones. Instead of moving forward when the light turns green after you have waited for eons for it to change, they are on their phones and not paying attention. Or the ones you get stuck behind when they're going ten miles per hour under the speed limit. When I am impatient, I am frustrated, judgmental, and not being very loving. My loving back-seat driver, the Holy Spirit, gently reminds me to love. I can choose to flip the switch. When I do, my heart changes. Instead of thinking how inconsiderate other drivers are being, I allow love to remind me about compassion and grace.

I am reminded first that there have been times I, too, was going too slow or failed to react to a green light. Their actions that frustrate me are no worse than my actions that frustrate others. This is grace in action.

Second, I recognize they are inhabitants of planet earth. People deal with many hardships, bad days, meanness of others, aching bodies, and so forth. They might just be having a hard day. I've had some of those. This is compassion in action.

Last, I do a 180. I think about the opposite of my fleshly response. In this situation, the appropriate response is to pray for the person. This is love in action.

We can apply this concept to every situation in our lives. It is especially helpful in relationships. By walking in the Spirit, we can love spouses, children, parents, bosses, co-workers, friends, neighbors, and even enemies. Flip the switch and walk in grace, compassion, and love.

Whether we are encouraging someone who is down or arguing with someone, if we speak in love and walk in the Spirit, love wins. Love is the God force, remember? When we avoid speaking in our flesh, we allow the Spirit to work in the situation. And this not only produces intimate and trusting relationships, but it also generates tremendous joy and peace. Even if things don't go as we want or expect, we can stand in peace knowing we did what God asked us to do. We loved.

The key to making this work is faith. We must have faith that God's plan of loving others is going to work out best for all involved. We must trust Him even if the person we are interacting with doesn't respond in love and the problem remains unresolved. Love does no harm to anyone. Love heals, brings life, and has an eternal effect.

If you struggle to love others, pray that the Lord would reveal to you your newly made heart. Ask Him to help you to look at people's spirit rather than their flesh and to know that you *can* love them by the power of the Holy Spirit. Ask that He would help you to choose compassion, grace, and forgiveness rather than hatred, judgment, and resentment. Pray He would help you submit to Him, walk in love, and help you be sensitive to the Spirit's nudging you to switch to the Light in moments when you are walking in your flesh.

When you recognize you are in your flesh, you can do a 180. When someone is trying to entice you to get in your flesh, either refuse to let your flesh take control or walk away. If your flesh is taunting you and you are struggling to feel valuable, go serve the undervalued. If you are tempted to judge someone, think of all the wonderful attributes they possess. You can love in the face of others' hate because you have the power of the Spirit of God living in you.

And when you fail, don't beat yourself up for stumbling. You are simply a human who still wrestles with your old sinful flesh, but remember, the real *you* is godly, righteous, holy, and capable of loving even the most difficult people by the Spirit. That sin is no longer put on your account! Don't waste your time with shame. Christ died for that. His grace is His love in action. And by His radical grace, we can put love into action too.

CHAPTER 17

The Freedom

Grace enables freedom.

The lights are flashing red and blue, and you suddenly feel like you have a rock in the pit of your stomach. The officer approaches your window, and you roll it down, reluctantly.

"May I have your license, registration, and proof of insurance, please?"

No one likes to hear those words, which send us frantically digging through the taco sauce packets and crumpled napkins in our glove compartment to find the documents buried within. But we dig anyway because it is the law.

We need laws so we can live safely as a society. Laws allow us to live together without infringing on the rights of others. And that works, for the most part. We could do better, but we could do a great deal worse.

But are laws all-or-nothing? Absolute? Or is there some wiggle room when it comes to their obedience? For example, would there ever be a reason to go 85 mph down a freeway with a posted limit of 75 mph? Or how about 25 mph? Of course, there is! You might speed to avoid an accident as someone is coming at you from behind, for a medical emergency, or because traffic is flowing at a higher speed, and it is safer for you to keep up. Likewise, we might go drastically under the speed limit if it's very foggy, or if there is a traffic jam in front of you, or because there is a herd of wild horses on the road – something I actually experienced myself once.

Frequently there are extenuating circumstances influencing our obedience to the laws of our land. In these situations, we do more good by not obeying the law than obeying it. We save lives. The law is designed to apply to *typical* circumstances. And if conditions allow, we need to obey these limits to maintain a peaceful society and the safety of our neighbors.

But is it the same for the law of God? Obeying the Ten Commandments or trying to live up to the CODE limits us, but can we accomplish much more by not limiting ourselves? For example, we can *not* steal from someone. Great! We didn't break the commandment. But what if we went beyond the bar of not stealing, and gave something like a helping hand, a bag of groceries, or an encouraging word to our neighbor? Wouldn't that be what "love your neighbor" is all about?

Jesus removed our limits. He made it so we can do much more than be obedient to rules and laws. He made it possible for us to be free. We have already discussed many of these freedoms. We are free from sin. No longer is our sin put on our account. We are forgiven. In Christ, we are free from the suppression and defeat of sin, the law, shame, and guilt. Grace has rescued us from being limited by our sin.

We have also talked about the fact that we can now walk in the Spirit and love others. Thanks to grace, we are freed from the control of our old sinful nature and free to put on our new spiritual nature.

These are amazing gifts, but I want to explore a couple more freedoms we receive in Christ. They are the freedom to identify as our new selves, and the freedom to be authentic.

Now that you are a follower of Christ, you are free to identify with the new you, your spiritual nature. You can live your life as dead to your flesh and alive to God in Christ. You can identify as a righteous, accepted, holy, and a loving child of God. You have been born into this new identity and can walk in it every day.

You can identify with the new spiritual you. Your identity is who God says you are in Christ. Take His word to heart. He calls you His child, a royal priesthood, a friend of Jesus and a citizen of the heavenly kingdom. You are His workmanship, a new creation and more than a conqueror. You are the salt of the earth and the light of the world.

Your new spiritual self is the light that shines and brings glory to God.

How do you let that light shine? You walk according to the Spirit. You are now free to *not* walk in your flesh but rather walk in the Spirit because Christ made you more than a conqueror. Conquerors go in and destroy the enemy so the king can enter the city. Jesus destroyed our enemy, sin, so we, the royal priesthood, the children of the King, don't have to conquer it. We can walk right into the righteous spiritual Kingdom of God and His love and keep walking in it. That's who you are. That is who you can identify as now.

When who we are on the inside is clear to us, we can make that clear to others. Your new internal identity allows you to be authentic externally. You are free to be that authentic you. You don't have to hide from who you are. No more running from yourself. Aslan put it beautifully in C.S. Lewis' *Prince Caspian*.

"You doubt your value. Don't run from who you are."

You are free to be you. You know you still have that old sinful flesh hanging around until you get to cut him or her loose, but your true identity is your new self. That is who you really are. That is who God created you to be when you were born again by the Spirit. That is the authentic you that you can reveal to others. That old man or woman doesn't lead the show anymore. Let the new you out of the box.

This idea has been quite a journey for me. As I've shared with you already, for most of my life I tried to run from who I was, but that was because I misunderstood who I was. I know now that I can't run from the old fleshly me because I keep dragging her around. But I can ignore her as I live in the newly remodeled righteous version of me. It took me a long time to learn this, but now I know who I am in Jesus. I can be authentic, both with myself and with others.

In recent years I have come to realize that when I meet new people, I can be my true self. I am determined now to allow the Spirit to help me live in righteousness, and we do pretty well together most of the time. But I also know that my old flesh sits up and takes over sometimes too. That's who I am. I am altogether whole and beautiful as well as broken and muddy. I am no longer going to try to hide my ugly side. I don't think it is beneficial to anyone for me to flaunt it for no reason, but if you see me mad, or selfish, or impatient, then I am not going to go curl up in a ball under my covers for days like I used to. You can accept me for who I am or not. I'm okay with your decision.

And, just so you know, I will accept you for who you are. Warts, failures, selfishness, love, grace, beauty, talents, sense of humor, lack of sense of humor, and all. No judgment here. I choose to be authentic because I cannot keep running from myself anymore. And I choose to accept you authentically too, knowing that that old man or woman is not who you really are.

We live in a world where we are afraid to be vulnerable with each other. Sometimes it's prudent to be a little closed off, but generally, we should be able to be ourselves without condemnation and judgment. Let's get back to God's plan of loving, supporting, and serving one another.

Just think how that would change our world if we

could be authentic with each other. Have you ever had any of these thoughts?

I don't understand why they can't just be real with me.

I wish they would just admit what they did and apologize.

Why can't they just talk to me and share what they are really feeling?

I have had those thoughts. I can't change the world, so I have decided to do to others what I wish they would do for me and allow my true self to exist. If you ask my opinion, I'll give it. If you see my flaws, that's ok. Let me know if I'm doing something that is hurtful to you. Be honest with me. I'll be honest with you. And in doing so, I need to trust that God has my back if I allow myself to be vulnerable with others and allow them to see the real me. I have fought doing this most of my life until deciding it was time for a change, time to rest. I have become tired of the pretense.

We are no longer limited to seeing ourselves through the lens of our failures. That isn't who we are anymore. We are free to be the new authentic us. While we see the unrighteousness of our flesh, we also see the righteousness of our new selves. We can be authentic because radical grace says we are not limited to our sinful flesh. We have been set apart from that old guy or gal and our identity is our newly made selves in Christ.

Will you take hold of these freedoms? Will you identify as a righteous child of God? What will you do with your liberty to love? You have the rest of your earthly stay to explore your boundless freedom in Christ.

I'm not talking about cheap grace and I'm not saying our freedom means we should do whatever our flesh wants, no matter the consequences. Grace isn't cheap. Jesus paid a huge price for our freedom. However, grace does mean we are free. Grace is radical because it produces that freedom. Both Peter and Paul understood how liberating our new freedom is. They both warned us not to use our freedom to cover up sin.

And freedom doesn't mean you should break our country's laws. Those laws, as I mentioned, are set up so we can live together harmoniously. If you base your actions in love, you will know that breaking the law for selfish reasons is not loving. Sometimes we must break it for the safety of others, as I explained before, but outside of those special circumstances, it is loving to obey the laws of our land. Even if we disagree with them.

What about God's law? The Ten Commandments, or the other six hundred-plus laws? Remember, we are no longer under the Jewish law. We are not bound by it. We are commanded by God to fulfill His new law of love. That means everything we do should be in love.

We can look at the Ten Commandments in light of the New Covenant and see that they are all about love. We can fulfill them through love. Don't take other people's stuff. That's not loving. Don't lie to them or testify falsely in court saying someone did something they didn't do. That's not loving. Don't wish you had what they have.

Do the loving thing and be happy for them. But fulfilling the law is not our mission now. It is just a great consequence that happens when we love one another like Jesus asked us to do.

Some teach that we are to obey the law or live by the CODE because we will be judged for our works. Now, usually they are careful to say that our judgment isn't to decide eternal damnation or not, but for rewards. They are sadly misinformed because, as Paul tells us in his letters, the law can only show us that we can't fulfill it. The Jewish nation couldn't, so why do we think we can? And if we only partially fulfill it, we have still broken it. The law can only bring about wrath because when we try to obey it, we become transgressors, or lawbreakers which is the very reason Jesus fulfilled it for us and freed us from its wrath.

I submit to you that there is a better way to accomplish good works. Stop focusing on your sin and old self and start walking in your new spiritual self. Love! Love your family. Serve them. Provide for them in an honest way. Love your community and love those that are difficult to love. When you do these things, there is no law against them. Grace removes the limits and gives us the possibility of unlimited love. Don't love for rewards, love because you can.

Some folks say that if you teach grace to people, they will sin even more than before they received grace. I repeat: you didn't need God's grace and mercy to influence you to sin before you knew Jesus. It is your flesh, tempted by the devil, that entices you to sin, and since you still carry around that old guy or gal, you will be tempted to sin until you die. We are tempted, but we aren't locked into having to go there. Radical grace means that in those moments, we are not alone. God tells us He will always give us a way to escape falling into the devil's trap.

Our flesh is stubborn. Some people struggle with addiction or mental illness or emotional strife. Some people are overwhelmed by things that might seem insignificant to most people. Living on this planet is very difficult, and we need help sometimes. We most certainly need to surround ourselves with people who are loving and supportive. If you don't feel like you have help and support, I beg you to find people who can be there for you. I know that without the help and support of my hubby, I never would have gotten through the very difficult things we got through.

I also know that learning about God's radical grace and how much He loves me, how free He made me, and how love is my purpose, helped me to rise above the depression, agoraphobia, OCD, suicidal thoughts, anger, and fear that plagued me for years. Radical grace has done this for me, and it will do it for you! You are free to be who God created you to be and because of that, you are limitless.

CHAPTER 18

The Forgiveness

Grace forgives.

I think I was born with a "KICK ME" sign on my back. I'm kicked so often that it has become a running joke in my family.

"It's the KICK ME sign again."

It seems like all my life I have dealt with people treating me badly. Even electronics and household items blitz out on me for no apparent reason. Sometimes the problems are not just inconveniences but are actually very hurtful. But even if it's something minor, like wait staff at restaurants serving everyone's food but mine, I am often reminded that it seems I have a "KICK ME" sign permanently affixed on me for all to see.

Thankfully I laugh about this running joke now. I didn't used to.

I can remember feeling like I was wearing a "KICK ME" sign even as a young child. When I was turning 7 my mom and I planned a wonderful birthday party for me. I sent out my *Birthday Party and Sleep Over* invitations to several of my girlfriends from school and waited eagerly for the day to arrive.

My mom splurged this time, which was a big deal because most years she couldn't afford to make such a fuss. The day of the party, a card table held Raggedy Ann paper plates and cups along with oranges that had candy canes stuck in them as straws, and the family room was adorned with matching crepe paper decorations and red balloons. I was tickled with anticipation. Mom went all out, and I was ready to reap the benefits of her efforts. I was going to have a blast! That Friday evening, I waited...and waited.

No one showed up.

Not a one.

I felt kicked in the stomach. I reasoned, since it was the beginning of Christmas break (my birthday is just a few days before Christmas), that was why they didn't show. Why they didn't tell me they weren't able to make it, I will never know. To feel better, the story I told myself was that they *had* to go with their families out of town for Christmas vacation. We have an instinct to soften blows with new narratives.

I know you have had your fair share of kicks in your life, and I want this chapter to speak to you about those times people have hurt you. I also want to share with you my journey of learning to deal with people who hurt me.

After being "kicked" by people, and life in general, a million times, I have learned about forgiveness. While the narrative helps soften the blow, forgiveness heals the wound. We all have someone to forgive, and if we have been forgiven by our gracious God, we can forgive others and be healed.

I can forgive the young girls who ghosted me for my birthday party, those who were mean to me in junior high, and wait-staff who are rude or neglectful. We can easily forgive people in these types of situations. But it is much harder to forgive people who hurt us deeply, especially if they are close friends or family.

When I started learning about God's forgiveness and our sin, I began to see something that made me realize why we all have a "KICK ME" sign pinned to our backs. It's because we all also have an "I'M GOING TO KICK YOU" sign hidden in our pockets. We don't *mean* to hurt other people, but we often end up doing just that. That's because we get into our flesh, and we make mistakes.

Some of us have hurt people more than others, but the point is that we have all sinned. We have all failed, in our flesh, to reach the standard of the glory of God.

This concept means we are all on the same *sin* playing field. Thankfully, though, Jesus has taken us to a new field. He has placed His followers on the *forgiven* playing field. No matter what you have done, or I have done, we are forgiven if we place our faith in His righteousness for our own. In our spiritual nature, no one is more, or less, righteous than anyone else.

This concept shook me when I learned it because I realized that from God's perspective, the people who had hurt me the most in my life are just as forgiven as I am if they have given their lives to Jesus. I wasn't sure I wanted that to be true, to be honest with you, because I felt like they didn't "deserve" forgiveness because of how much they had hurt me. That was my flesh speaking, of course.

I realized I was being like Jonah. He didn't want to go to Nineveh and preach repentance because he knew that God would forgive the people of Nineveh for their wickedness because He is a gracious God. Jonah became angry in his self-righteousness. After a trip out to sea and a short stint in the belly of a fish, he came to his senses. I did too, eventually; fortunately, without having to occupy the inside of Moby Dick first.

The Spirit reminded me that I had been forgiven much, so I decided that I could forgive as well. I *chose* to forgive. Forgiveness is the loving thing to do. It is what we do if we are a child of God. It did take a while for me to grapple with forgiving the two men who had hurt me so severely. But eventually, it wasn't that I *had* to forgive, it was that I *wanted* to forgive.

God's grace evens the playing field. Grace makes it possible for forgiveness to happen.

When I started down this process, and it is a process, to forgive my most guilty offenders, it was very difficult. I had been sexually abused by two men whom I should have been able to trust. The damage they did to me was catastrophic. It tore huge holes in me. It wrecked me. The consequences of their sin also affected my later relationships and the way I responded to the world around me. I was angry most of the time. The anger overwhelmed me and bound me in depression.

I am an artist and when I reflect on the artwork that I produced during that time I see my anger oozing out. One time I created a painting that was the view of my forehead with a tiger leaping out of my head, baring its fangs and claws. I felt as if I had a roaring monster in my mind. I knew the only way to rid myself of this destructive feeling was to forgive.

I reminded myself daily of the fact that those men are on the same field as me. I thought about the fact that God could forgive them like He forgave me. I knew they struggled. I knew their stories.

I would pray many times per day for God to help me forgive them and have compassion for them. I asked God to help me lay down the anger I had because it was getting in the way of forgiveness. Once I knew about my dual natures, I would recognize that my anger and bitter heart were in my flesh and that I could step into the Spirit and see them the way God saw them. It started with developing compassion for them. I even prayed they would give themselves to Jesus. That sounds strange, or radical, but God's grace is radical, right?

This process took several years. Slowly, the thought of them and the damage they caused me came to my mind less often. As I healed through the help of the Holy Spirit, my husband, and learning about God's grace, it became evident to me that forgiveness was a natural consequence of understanding His grace.

In fact, years later, I found out that one of the men who hurt me had given himself to Jesus. At first, I felt a little Jonah-ish.

But my awesome *in*sidekick, the Holy Spirit, whispered to me, *"That's a good thing."*

Yeah, I know. It is.

And I *had* asked for it. It was another testimony of God's radical grace.

Are your kickers saved? If so, they are forgiven. That is a good thing. Forgive them and pray for them. Are your kickers unsaved? If so, forgive them and pray for them. But please know that forgiveness of someone who has done as destructive things to you as the men in my life did to me doesn't mean you have to go to dinner with them and give them a big hug. Forgiveness is different than relationship. Only you and God can define that relationship once you forgive.

Since going through the process of forgiving my worst offenders, it has become much easier to forgive people who hurt me. That "KICK ME" sign is still attached to me, so I must make forgiveness a regular occurrence. Of course, it's easy to forgive the minor, petty wrongs. It is less easy to forgive the deeper and more hurtful transgressions, but I press on in the knowledge that forgiveness is necessary. I don't ever want to go back to being that angry, fearful Jonah again.

What about you? Are there some people who have hurt you deeply? I pray you can see God's gracious perspective of your wrongdoers. I pray you can begin that process of forgiveness and healing, not only because it is love in action, but also because it will free you from the tigers in your head. Forgiveness liberates us from some of the destructive consequences of our painful experiences so we can focus on allowing God to heal the rest.

Radical grace forgives.

CHAPTER 19

The Gospel of (Radical) Grace

By grace we have been saved, and that's just the beginning!

Mary Sanford was born in 1623 in England and died in 1662 in the town of Hartford in the Connecticut colony. Mary was my 9th great-grandmother. She was hanged at 39 years of age.[7]

I love to research my ancestry. I am blessed to have a great deal of information available to me that goes back a very long time, and my research has led me to discover some interesting things. For example, I probably came from Vikings, am a descendant of the King and Queen of Wales and might even be related to Lady Godiva. But none of those peoples' stories are as intriguing to me as my 9x-great-grandmother Mary from Connecticut.

At some point after her birth, she made it from England to the fledgling colonies of the New World. She married Andrew Sanford and while living in Hartford, when Mary was 20 years old, they had a baby boy and gave him his father's name, Andrew Jr.

By 1662 the Puritan community in which they lived had been holding witch trials for 15 years.[7] The Connecticut witch trials came well before the famous trials of

Salem, Massachusetts which began in 1692. The witch trials were a sad and devastating time in our country's history.

The Puritans lived by their religious laws that they had created based on what they believed were Biblical. They believed that people were either chosen to be saved, or they were not chosen to be saved. If you were not chosen, there was no way you could be saved. You couldn't confess, repent, promise, say you'll change, go to jail for a while, or pay your way to salvation. It was a graceless theology that was the basis for their reasoning as to why they had to kill those whom they found guilty of witchcraft.

Why couldn't they just leave those people alone and let them be? I would guess it is because they feared that the "witches" might cast spells on people and cause pain or suffering. We all respond to fearful, or seemingly fearful, situations by either fleeing or standing against that which causes us to be afraid. This is called the fight or flight response. The Puritans chose to fight.

Sometimes, the way they rendered a verdict was to throw the alleged witch, bound, into a lake. If the accused floated, they reasoned, it was witchcraft that saved them from drowning. And if they sank, they were absolved – too late for many of them, of course, since by that point they had drowned.[7] Other times the leaders based their verdict on the testimony of people in the community, which was fraught with problems because a neighbor motivated by ill will, could fabricate evidence to condemn someone.

Both Mary and Andrew were accused of witchcraft in 1662. Someone had seen Mary with other accused women dancing under a tree and enjoying a bottle of wine. Both Andrew and Mary were indicted for having "dealings with Satan" and for holding meetings that weren't prescribed by the leaders of the community.[7]

During their trial, there were mixed opinions amongst the leaders and townspeople concerning their guilt. It was common at the time for men who were accused of witchcraft to avoid conviction. In the end, Andrew was acquitted, but Mary was not.

If it weren't for her one son, Andrew Jr., I would not exist. Mind-blowing, right?

The leaders of the community didn't believe in free will choice for salvation. Their beliefs came from the 16th century theology of John Calvin. Their beliefs led them to kill alleged sinners rather than preach the gospel to them because they believed those sinners were a lost cause. This exemplifies what a religious practice looks like when it is devoid of grace. They didn't believe people could accept Jesus even if they told them about Him, and the women they convicted weren't given a chance because they were *obviously* not one of the chosen. The community didn't preach the gospel; they abandoned it.

I honestly don't know if Mary was practicing witch-craft or not. She might have just loved to dance and went to the woods to do it so no one would judge her. She might have had a deep relationship with Jesus. Maybe she was dancing as an act of worship. Only God truly knows. But had the other members of her community believed in what the Bible says about salvation and God's grace, they would have loved her, talked with her, invited her to receive Jesus if she hadn't yet, prayed over her, and respected her decision to receive Jesus or not. This is a great example of looking at another person's actions and assuming the status of their heart based on those actions. This is a dangerous practice that has existed since the dawn of humanity.

The church has endured many interpretations of the Bible and the Gospel of Grace over the millennia. This is possible because not everyone reads the Bible for themselves, and they depend on teachers to tell them what the Bible says. People come and go with their version of the truth and others follow. Having said that, I urge you to see for yourself if what I present in this book is supported by the Bible. I base everything I talk about on the Bible, interpreting it through grace with Jesus at the center of it, and I always consider the broader context of any verse I examine. And remember, I have included an appendix in the back of this book, for your review, that contains the references to every scripture that I paraphrase or Biblical topic that I discuss.

Over the last eighteen chapters, I have reviewed a large portion of the Gospel of Grace. I have established the foundation of the Gospel while trying to refute some of the false teachings that have complicated the Gospel of

Grace for centuries. I have tackled topics such as legalism, our dual natures, the absence of the grace of God, and teaching about the Holy Spirit's role in our daily lives.

I believe it is now time to simply lay out the Gospel of Grace in its entirety. When we fully receive it in its pure form, without it being tainted by the virus of legalism or the lack of the Holy Spirit, it is quite simple and truly good news.

I have years of experience teaching Sunday school as well as several adult ministries. One approach to teaching the Gospel that I have seen is a simplified "ABC": Accept. Believe. Confess. I have also heard a more complex version of it called the Romans Road, which only cites verses from the Book of Romans. It doesn't matter what method is used to remember the elements of the Gospel. The important thing is to know it personally and thoroughly. If you understand and believe its components, you can live in the freedom that God's grace offers, and you will be able to share that message of freedom with others because it will be a personal testimony.

The Gospel is straightforward in that it is all about Jesus, who He is, and what He has done for us. It is simple because it only requires us to do one thing: put our faith *in* Jesus. However, the Gospel is also complex in that it involves many elements that can't be boiled down to a three-letter acronym on a children's Sunday school paper. These are the elements I have been exploring with you over the past eighteen chapters. It is time to put everything together.

I realize that going over the Gospel might be a review for you, but I want to make sure you get the *Radical Grace* version.

I have never been completely satisfied with any version of the Gospel I have encountered because I felt there was always some part of it missing. The following is the Gospel of (Radical) Grace using scriptures from the Book of Romans, but unlike the typical Romans Road version, I have added some verses that are important. I think they are a significant part of the Gospel and must be incorporated. If you understand each component in the list and believe it is true, it should be life-changing, and you will be able to easily share the Gospel of Grace with others. My comments follow the verses.

Romans 3:23. ...for all have sinned and fall short of the glory of God.

Because of what Adam did, everyone is born into unrighteousness, and therefore born into sin. Your unrighteousness is very important to recognize. No one can enter eternity if they are unrighteous.

Romans 6:23. For the wages of sin is death, but the gift of God is eternal life in Christ Jesus our Lord.

The penalty for your sin is death. Jesus offers you eternal life.

Romans 5:8. But God demonstrates His own love toward us, in that while we were still sinners, Christ died for us.

Because of His great love and grace, Christ died to pay that penalty for you.

Romans 10:9. ...that if you confess with your mouth the Lord Jesus and believe in your heart that God has raised Him from the dead, you will be saved.

If you believe and confess Jesus is who He says He is and did what He says He did, you will be saved. Your mouth speaks what is in your heart.

Romans 10:10. For with the heart one believes unto righteousness, and with the mouth confession is made unto salvation.

By your faithful confession, you receive both the righteousness of Christ and His salvation, which is eternal life with Him. You cannot receive salvation without righteousness.

Romans 10:4. For Christ is the end of the law for righteousness to everyone who believes.

You are no longer bound by the law. You cannot make yourself righteous by obeying the law. Jesus imputes His righteousness to those who have faith in Him.

Romans 6:14. For sin shall not have dominion over you, for you are not under law but under grace.

You are no longer bound by sin. Your old man or woman has no grip on the new you. The law gave sin its power, but Jesus fulfilled the law and brought an end to trying to fulfill it, so sin lost its control.

Romans 13:14. But put on the Lord Jesus Christ, and make no provision for the flesh, to fulfill its lusts.

You now have two natures. You can put off your old fleshly self and put on your new spiritual self. You can live a life defined by your new holy nature in Christ while you cast off the life defined by your failures and flesh. Refuse your flesh the opportunity to fulfill its desires by walking in your new spirit nature.

Romans 7:6. But we now have been delivered from the law, having died to what we were held by, so that we should serve in the newness of the Spirit and not in the oldness of the letter.

You now serve God by the Holy Spirit not by obeying the letter of the law. You have a new life that isn't characterized by the old law but by love.

Romans 13:10. Love does no harm to a neighbor; therefore love is the fulfillment of the law.

Love is the goal of God's law. Love is the New Covenant law.

Romans 8:4. ...that the righteous requirement of the law might be fulfilled in us who do not walk according to the flesh but according to the Spirit.

The Spirit empowers you to walk in Him and to love others. There is no law against love.

Romans 8:5. For those who live according to the flesh set their minds on the things of the flesh, but those who live according to the Spirit, the things of the Spirit.

If you set your mind on trying to subdue your flesh, then your whole life will be lived in your flesh, which is a waste because you are attempting to do what Jesus already did for you. Set your mind instead on things of the Spirit and walk in Him.

By grace we have been saved, and that's just the beginning!

There is a simple, streamlined way to state the Gospel of Grace:

If you put your faith in Jesus' righteousness for your own, then you will be saved, made righteous, and be equipped to live in that righteousness.

Once you fully grasp the Gospel of Grace, it won't matter how you present it to others. When you speak of God's radical grace through faith in Jesus for your own life, that testimony will impact those around you. Make the Gospel your own and share His glory with others when they ask why you have hope.

One final thought: The Gospel is simple in that it can be stated simply, but all aspects of it must be understood entirely in their Biblical truth. I have heard false gospels preached that either leave out elements of the true

Gospel of Grace or add things that aren't true. Either way is damaging and dangerous. The doctrine that my 9th great-grandmother must have heard was sadly lacking. That version surely left out grace in almost every way God gives it to us, as well as how we give it to others.

We have a loving God who bankrupted heaven by sending His Son, Jesus, to give His life for ours. Our response to His love is faith in Him and what He did for us and a deep love for God. By understanding the complete Gospel of Grace, and how radical it really is, I pray you are blessed by His goodness and grace. Grab hold of Jesus and His truly good news! Hold it tight and never let go! Jesus did what He did because He wants you to live a life that is marked by hope, joy, and peace. He wants you to live free and unashamed! Let go of the false teachings that drag you down and step into your new life in Christ!

CHAPTER 20

The Foundation

Grace is the footing for our souls.

"I just want to go Home."

That is what my mother said when I asked her what she wanted for Christmas. It was November of 2007, and I was finishing up my Christmas shopping right before our family was to be traveling to Arizona to see my parents. We wouldn't be able to visit during Christmas, so we were going to celebrate it a little early during our trip for Thanksgiving.

My mother had had breast cancer and the mastectomy left her with painful nerve damage. Not only that, but the damage made her hand unable to grip at times. She would drop things unexpectedly. She had many health issues and was miserable in her body. She wanted to go to her eternal home. I can't say I blamed her for wanting to spend Christmas with the birthday boy. I could certainly sympathize.

A few days later it was time to pack. We usually made the trip with our spacious travel trailer so that our family of five wouldn't overcrowd my parents in their little house in the hills of Pinal County. The day before our trip was the busiest for me as I finished up loading the SUV and trailer with toys, gifts, and some Thanksgiving groceries we were tasked with bringing.

After I finished packing, I took a break in my glider rocker that sat by the window in the living room. I needed to sit for a while and rest my weak back before finishing my other tasks for the day. I was worn out and feeling gloomy. I found myself staring out the window, overwhelmed with sorrow. I couldn't shake the feeling, but as any mom can attest, I had to keep going, there was still more to do. So, after some time, I got going again. We had to be ready to take off the next morning.

That evening my dad called. He informed me that Mom hadn't felt well earlier that afternoon. When he called the doctor and described how she was feeling, the doctor told him to get her to the hospital right away. Not long after being admitted, an aneurism in her brain burst, and she passed away. She had lost all blood pressure, closed her eyes, and went to go see Jesus.

I experienced a weird mixture of emotions. I was so terribly sad, but also happy for her that God had given her the one thing she wanted for His birthday. She would never again have to deal with her body not working right, but I was heartbroken. My emotions are still very split over her death. I miss her greatly and wish I could call her up and talk like we used to, give her a hug, or be silly and laugh with her, but I am so glad she was able to be released from the harshness the world inflicted upon her during the nearly 67 years of her stay.

My mother knew that when she died, she would be

welcomed by Jesus. Because of God's grace and love for her she trusted Him and put herself in His arms. She didn't fear death. She desired it because her earthly body had given out on her. Grace was the reason why she could not only face death but see it as better than life here on earth. She was drawn to God and desired to be with Him.

Some people fear that once they are standing before God in eternity, He is going to deal with them based on their "good" or "bad" works, not by His grace. They think God will either go easy on them or be harsh with them based on what they did while on earth. They believe their works will determine whether they are punished or not, or to what degree they will be punished. The truth is we are only judged by our acceptance of or refusal of the Gospel of Grace.

John says something amazing in First John chapter four. He tells us that we can be bold in the day of judgment and that God's perfect love casts out our fears. He goes on to say that the reason we love Him is because He loved us first. That love is why God gives us grace. We can trust His love and grace. John goes on to say that God's love is what draws us in to Him, not our ability to obey. Just love. That's it. It is His love that draws us in, not our obedience to the law or the CODE. Before we get to heaven God does chasten or teach us through our sinful mistakes and their corresponding consequences, but His punishment is reserved for people who refuse His offer of salvation by His grace.

Oh, the fullness and radical reach of His grace!

When we fully grasp God's love considering His grace, we can live freely without fear of punishment or eternal judgment. We will be able to stand before Him and say, "Yes, I made mistakes all the time. Only You know how truly terrible my failures have been. But I am your child and Your Son, Jesus, has redeemed me. I know You love me. You said I can come boldly to your throne without fear, so here I am."

Radical grace is the footing for our souls. It is the basis upon which we are drawn to God and needn't fear Him once we stand before Him. It is the foundation that, like Mom, we should all rest our lives upon. When we do that, we will be excited about meeting Him, and when we are faced with death, we will be able to say, "I want to go Home."

Mom was free from the fear of death and facing her Creator because she knew He accepted her for who she was. Because of God's acceptance, we don't need to fear death, but we also don't need to base our value on whether others accept us or not. We don't need to strive to impress people to know that we have value. We can live confidently knowing that our value comes from God.

Here is a story to demonstrate how we taught our children the lesson about not basing their value on what others think of them.

Our family loves food from Schlotzsky's Deli. The

children grew up eating there often because it was located next door to our church. We would go for lunch after church, or before a Home School Co-op class because it was convenient, and we would usually see people we knew in our small community. They always had great music playing and it was a nice atmosphere. Not to mention there was a TCBY located in the restaurant which the kids frequented. Not me, I saved my calories for coffee flavored ice cream with toffee or chocolate chips.

One time we were all sitting at a table enjoying a meal. A peppy song came over the speakers and my husband and children started bobbing their heads off to one side, in time with the music and each other. They were so silly looking. They encouraged me to join in the silliness. I resisted for a few beats but soon joined in the fun.

As parents we always wanted to teach our children not to be man-pleasers and need others' approval. We wanted them to know that God accepts them for who they are, and they don't need to impress others for validation. They could be themselves and not worry about what others thought of them. Phillip was the instigator of these silly moments to enforce this idea. We had many hilarious and would-be embarrassing moments, but we didn't care. The kids learned not to care if people thought we were weird. I'm sure some people still think the Appel family is weird. And that's okay.

Of course, it came back to bite Phillip. It has been many years since those silly days of trying to embarrass our kids. He was recently reminded of his lessons by our now-grown son. Phillip had been having some issues with his legs and found relief by wearing compression socks. I am talking about thin black socks that go up to his knees. You must understand, he wears shorts every season, no matter the temperature. Those socks with shorts and running shoes look a little weird if you have any sense of fashion.

Our son and his family were visiting on a day that Phillip was dressed in his strange compression sock outfit. Before leaving the house with our son to pick up lunch, Phillip said, "Hang on a minute, I'm going to change my socks."

To which our son replied, "What, Dad, are you embarrassed?"

Touché.

Phillip laughed. They left right away to get lunch with great memories in mind and Phillip's socks remained in place.

Our son had learned the lesson. You can receive it too. Because of grace, you can be the real you. God accepts you and loves you knowing your flaws. You can be authentic. Even when you are dorky. The socks you choose to wear (compression or otherwise), the hobbies you choose to participate in, and the silly things you say and do are a beautiful picture of who you really are. You can be you without being embarrassed. You are exactly who God made you to be. You don't need to impress others, or God. He loves you just the way you are. God's love and grace are the bedrock that allows you to stand firmly and confidently knowing that you have value no matter what others think of you.

We can live confidently in God's radical grace, walk in freedom from fear, and trust that God treasures us dearly. We don't have to hide who we are from God or from others. When we are authentic, our lives are a testimony to the goodness of God. We can be honest and tell people that we are a hot mess, but God loves us anyway. His love is not based on what we do or don't do. Unfortunately, this message isn't what most of the world hears.

My mom once told me the reason we didn't go to church was because she saw church leaders posturing like they could do no wrong, then later in the week, she would see them doing things they would never admit to on Sunday morning, such as demeaning women or engaging in outbursts of anger. They were both living and preaching the emptiness of the CODE, knowing no one could master it, nor could they. Their hypocrisy convinced her to stay home and have a relationship with Jesus that was outside of the mixed message of the church. If they had just been real, would that have changed her perspective of church? Would I have received Jesus as a child? Thankfully God had a plan for me despite not going to church, but I wonder what I missed out on because we didn't go.

This hypocritical kind of witness is common because the typical messaging about God's grace is weak. And that message is weak because we are busy about trying to live up to the CODE while hiding our failure to do so, instead of walking freely in God's grace. Living legalistically according to the law or the CODE, as I have touched on already, tends to draw us into judgmentalism and anger, or even hatred toward others, as we place an unachievably high standard on them. What sort of message are we telling the unsaved world when we are unloving and judgmental toward them because they are disobedient sinners? That message clearly declares that because of their sin, they are not accepted by us or God.

Often our lives reflect the fact that we really don't get God's grace. We have accepted that weak message ourselves, so that is what we pass on to others. We tend to be dishonest about our own failures because we want others to accept us and not judge us. But we aren't fooling anyone; the unsaved world reads us loud and clear. This empty messaging makes them say things like,

"Why would I want to be a Christian? Christians are hypocrites."

Everybody abhors hypocrisy, right? Don't you wish people would just be real with you? I have heard a lot of commentary, both online and in real life, about the hypocrisy of Christians. Many people hear the message, "Come to Jesus, just as you are, He loves you." Then the next thing they are told is that they need to stop sinning so much, just obey, and work on becoming more holy. But then they see the church putting on a façade, *pretend-*

ing that they can obey the CODE, and only putting their best side forward knowing full well they are a mess. People see right through this.

Hypocrisy is defined as saying one thing and doing another, and some believers embody this contradiction: they incorrectly assert they are living up to that standard while either demanding perfect obedience of others or shaming them for not meeting that bar. I know this is tough to hear, but as children of God, we need to face this and make it right.

How do we do that? How do we change the misperception of God's grace and preach the truth to the unsaved world? With authentic words and actions. The opposite of hypocrisy is authenticity. We need to be authentic. We need to be honest. And the only way we can be authentic is to accept God's radical grace for ourselves, walk in that grace, admit we are a mess, and preach the true Gospel that is founded on God's radical grace. We must stop preaching a gospel of some moral standard of unobtainable obedience while we pretend that the ones preaching that message are without sin.

When we live in the confidence that we can boldly stand before God because of what Jesus did for us, our lives preach about God's goodness and grace and that message will draw others to Him. It is not the anger or hatred of God that brings repentance. It is His goodness. And it is our mission as children of God to draw people into God's Kingdom, not push them away.

You stand on the foundation of Jesus and His grace. That grace is the reason you can be authentic and live without fear of meeting Him upon your death. You don't need to worry about what others think of you. From your goofy socks on the outside, to your zany and eccentric thoughts on the inside, God thinks you are amazing. And when you stand firmly on the foundation of grace, others will be amazed that you live a life of freedom and joy while being honest about who you are. When they ask you how you can live so freely even though you sin sometimes, you will be able to point them to the giver of that free and authentic life. In doing so, you will draw people to Jesus. Be who you are in God's radical grace and maybe try a little head bobbing the next time you are out to lunch.

CHAPTER 21

The Bootstrap Gospel

A gospel void of grace is no gospel at all.

"Pull yourself up by your bootstraps!"

Many boots have two pull straps, one on either side of the shaft, that are used to assist in pulling the boot over the heel. However, this absurd saying suggests that you could lift yourself *off the floor* by pulling on those straps. The literal idea of it is foolishness. Raising yourself off the floor by pulling on your own bootstraps cannot be done. It is impossible.

Figuratively, this saying speaks of mustering up some moxie and gumption to get yourself out of a difficult situation or an emotional pit. It instructs you to get going, stop wasting time, and start making things happen by your own effort, without the help of others.

This definition is why I dubbed a popular false gospel *The Bootstrap Gospel*, or *B.S. Gospel* for short. This doctrine teaches that you should pursue your sanctification and righteousness through your own effort, works, and obedience to the CODE, rather than resting in God's grace and knowing He already did these things for you. It is a concept that is so embedded in Christian culture you might not recognize it when it is presented to you. But you *must* recognize it because it is the opposite of grace. Any Christian message about salvation, sanctification, or everyday life based on works is void of grace and therefore is a false gospel. False doctrine is dangerous because it leads people away from God and can cause people to walk away from the church and their faith altogether.

The Bootstrap Gospel produces guilt, shame, and judgement toward yourself and others through the teaching of progressive sanctification. It also leaves out the concept of our dual natures and the ministry of the Spirit, which are all essential to allowing you to live the abundant and loving life Jesus wants you to live.

The problem with the B.S. Gospel is that it is based on legalistic efforts to try to be more Christlike and that it leaves out the Spirit from our everyday lives. As I have discussed, legalism leads to judgment, and disregarding the ministry of the Spirit in our daily lives directs us away from relying on Him to walk in love.

First, let's talk about legalism. Legalistic teachings encourage people to strive to work on their sinful nature through attempting to sin less and do better at being good. Teachers highlight the fact that people break the law of Moses or live a life of disobedience. Sin is usually the emphasis of these teachings.

Progressive sanctification is a type of legalistic teaching that also emphasizes sin. I have already explained progressive sanctification in a previous chapter, but I want to return to it in the context of the Bootstrap Gospel. This popular view of sanctification is an age-old attempt to deal with the fact that the followers of Christ still sin at times yet are supposed to be new creations. Progressive sanctification seeks to explain that even as a new creation, we still miss the mark because we are not holy yet. Without understanding our dual natures, this seems like a reasonable explanation. But this construct breaks down because it leaves out grace, denies the fact that the Bible says we are already sanctified, and focuses on our own works.

Advocates of progressive sanctification claim that if we do obey the CODE by doing good works and avoiding bad works, we gradually become more like Jesus. As you work on sinning less, with God's help, of course, you are making progress in your sanctification or taking steps toward being more holy, more Christlike. So, the theory goes.

In an earlier chapter, I explained that your new spiritual self is already holy, and you can't make your flesh holy, no matter what you do. Progressive sanctification denies this fact.

You can see why progressive sanctification is a major component of the Bootstrap Gospel. It claims you never will be completely holy until you die and go to heaven, but in the meantime, it is your job to try your best. It's your job to pull yourself up by your own bootstraps;

work on yourself to be "more Christlike."

According to advocates of this doctrine, if you simply rely on God to make you holy, you are being spiritually lazy and neglecting discipline. Therefore, you must play an active part in your sanctification. But even they admit that this approach can cause problems. They state if you overemphasize your participation in sanctification, that can lead to pride, self-righteousness, and legalism.

Let's explore this concept a little further.

How does this doctrine define what it means to be "more Christlike?" It is described as having more of the characteristics of Jesus. Specifically, though, how is "more" defined? Honestly, I can't find the answer. Putting our faith in Jesus and being born again has already given us the ability to be like Jesus when we walk according to the Spirit. Not *more* like Him but *like* Him. The Bible is clear that once we are born again, we have two natures that are totally separate. Our spirit is made alive in Christ and is already both holy and righteous.

If you do something righteous in any given moment, like be kind, loving, or patient, you are not being a little kind, or to a degree, kind. You *are* kind. You are not more loving in any given moment; you *are* loving. You are not mostly patient; you *are* patient. How can you be more patient? You either are patient, or you are not.

This doctrine teaches that you might accomplish being more patient if you are obedient, but what scale should you use? Is it a combined percentage based on how often you are patient versus how often you are impatient? Maybe you can be patient 75% of the time, and someday you might even get to 99%. But I submit to you, if you are patient for 3 seconds, then impatient for 1 second, you are not 75% patient; you were 100% patient for 3 seconds and 100% impatient for 1 more. There is no in-between. Think of it as digital, not analog; discrete, not continuous; on or off. It is binary: either/or, yes or no.

You were 100% patient for 3 seconds and 100% impatient for 1 second. And, the next time, you might be patient for only 1 millisecond, and not for the entire next week. But that doesn't mean you aren't holy. It means you were walking in the Spirit for a millisecond and then in your flesh.

Once we are in Christ, we can't walk in both our flesh and spirit at the same time. Our flesh and spirit aren't a mixture like mud that might be a little more water than dirt. Rather, they are separate. It is like trying to put one foot in Colorado and one in Minnesota at the same time. You just can't do it. Both feet walk together in the same state. Similarly, both of your feet walk together in the same nature. You are either in your flesh or in your spirit. Never both. But when you are in the Spirit, you are like Jesus.

Why is this important? So that you know you can walk *in* righteousness, and you don't condemn yourself when you fail to walk in it. Rather, you learn from it. Because of what Jesus did for you, you can do anything righteous and holy at any given moment. That's why He did what He did! He wanted you to be free from striving and working so you could love! That is the incredible news of the Gospel! You can switch on that Light because you are already sanctified, set apart for God, and holy. You are now free to love! No bootstrap yanking necessary.

Understanding this concept is the difference between being a New Covenant believer, a new creation, a citizen of the spiritual kingdom of God, freed from the law, walking in the Spirit, creating life and love around you, and not. Believing you are holy is believing the Gospel of Grace and living in it. Knowing God already made you like Jesus is all the difference in the world.

Like the proponents of progressive sanctification warn, the B.S. Gospel creates judgment, pride, and self-righteousness through comparison. As people work on becoming more Christlike by working on their sin, it is easy to start judging themselves and others based on how well they are progressing. If they fail at being good, they compare themselves to others and end up discouraged. If they succeed at being good, they too compare themselves to others and become prideful.

I did exactly this. Before I learned about God's radical grace, I struggled to see myself for the accepted child of God that I was. Meanwhile, I looked at others through the lens of their sin and bad behaviors. I was appalled by others' actions while I was striving to pull myself up in my own strength, blinded to my own faults.

That is how we get self-righteous Christians who repulse the unsaved world. Then those who are repulsed connect the self-righteousness of believers to the doctrine of the Christian faith and to Jesus Himself and don't want anything to do with Him.

Legalism teaches we must work on our sin and be obedient to the CODE to become holy. When we are focused on the law, the CODE, or trying to correct our sin we are walking in our flesh because our focus is on fleshly, nonspiritual, and unholy things. The Gospel of Grace, however, says although we are all sinners, those who are in Christ are sanctified. We are already made holy. We start at the cross and go up from there as we walk in His Spirit and in love. No judgment. No pride. No self-righteousness. Just grace.

Legalism is the first main problem with the Bootstrap Gospel. The second main problem with it is that the Spirit is often left out of the teaching or one of His ministries is over-emphasized to the point of neglecting the others.

I have rarely heard pastors teach about the Spirit. The Bootstrap Gospel doesn't know what to do with Him. Proponents of this work-reward system don't know what to do with scriptures such as the one in Romans that tells us we should "serve in the newness of the Spirit" (Rom 7:6). The doctrine of the B.S. Gospel is all about obeying the rules, so teachers ignore verses that speak of having been delivered from the law and mention walking in the Spirit.

By the power of the Spirit, we can serve in that newness. No striving is necessary. The Spirit is dwelling in you, producing fruit for you to give out to those around you and guiding you as you walk in Him. You just need to let Him lead the way!

When I discovered the miracle and purpose of the Spirit in my life, I began down the path to freedom from working on trying to be a better person through the CODE and trusting in the Spirit to guide my life. I held tight the idea of my new nature that communes with the Spirit. As I chose to walk in the Spirit, I realized that focusing on my sin and trying to fix myself was a distraction from doing the things God desires for me to do, such as serve, encourage, pray for, help, and care for others. These are the things that define what it means to love others.

Our new spiritual nature makes sense of the scriptures that talk about walking in the Spirit, no longer being under the law, and being a new creation. The Bootstrap Gospel doesn't include this essential truth.

If you are in Christ, you are already Christlike and holy in your new nature. You can let that part of you shine by walking in that truth. Walk in the Spirit. When you do things that are spiritual and based in love, then at that moment, you are 100% Christlike. No CODE or pulling on your bootstraps is needed. Just practice that walk. Even the apostle Paul knew it wasn't going to happen all the time, but he got back up and pressed on.

Because the Bootstrap Gospel denies you of your new nature and only focuses on your old nature of sin, it claims your goal is to make yourself more holy by sinning less. You will always be working toward something you cannot attain, and never feel like you have arrived at a place to start living life and loving others. When will that time be? How can you know when you are ready to move on if it is based on some measure of holiness that you can't really define? You are wasting your time you could be walking in holiness that is already defined for you. Keep in mind that walking in the Spirit isn't a check list or linear process you have to graduate through successfully as you master each step. Walking in love is possible at any moment. It is a way of life that creates beauty in the world around you, reconciliation, forgiveness, and redemption when you stop yanking on your bootstraps and simply walk in the new shoes Jesus put on your feet through His death and resurrection.

You can easily distinguish the Bootstrap Gospel from the Gospel of Grace. The Bootstrap Gospel emphasizes striving in your flesh to try to fix it through obedience to the law or the CODE, while the Gospel of Grace emphasizes the beauty of the new spiritual you that can walk in the leading of the Spirit and produce spiritual fruit.

The Bootstrap Gospel also generates shame as you struggle against your flesh and fail. However, the Gospel of Grace opens up infinite possibilities to experience godly, spiritual, life-giving, love-centered, grace-infused moments.

The Bootstrap Gospel swallows up your time and resources while you aimlessly work to better yourself. It is a dreary way of life because you are always working, never resting, and fearful of failure. But the Gospel of Grace sets you free and removes all limits so you can enjoy your life and relationships. You can daily rest in Jesus. You will enjoy what God does in your life with your faith that He really has done what He says He did for you. You are blessed by His work.

The Bootstrap Gospel traps you into an impossible quest for perfection that just leaves you frustrated. It says *Jesus is the standard of perfection, now go try to live up to Him*, all while knowing you never will. But Jesus says, *I am the standard of perfection and I'm giving that to you, now go and enjoy it.* It is all the difference in the world.

The Bible warns us to beware of false gospels. Paul in particular, warns us about false gospels. In the Book of Galatians, Paul explains that a different gospel isn't simply another gospel that is equally valid; rather, it is not a gospel at all.

Paul was concerned about legalism influencing the people of Galatia. They had believed false teachings that their righteousness would come through their own works rather than by the grace of God through faith in the righteousness of Jesus. Paul drives home the point that there is only one true gospel, which is the Gospel of Grace.

The word *gospel* means *good news*. If you hear a gospel that isn't such good news, then it isn't a gospel. I don't consider it good news to hear that it is my job as a believer to work hard the rest of my life trying to become a better person, since I know I would fail at the attempt. A gospel that is void of grace is no gospel at all.

Sometimes that *different gospel* is difficult to recognize because it is justified by scripture taken out of context. However, there is a key you can apply to anything to make sure it is indeed the valid message of the Gospel of Grace. Simply make sure Jesus and grace are in the middle of whatever you are hearing or reading. A gospel which includes Jesus but adds other conditions you must fulfill to achieve salvation or sanctification is a "Jesus + works" doctrine and is therefore false. We will look at other keys for evaluating the validity of any message or teaching in the next chapter.

The Bootstrap Gospel doesn't pull you into righteous living, it pulls you away from God's grace. Grace is such a beautiful thing. God's grace needs to be shouted from the rooftops! When you absolutely receive and understand God's radical grace, it will change you forever as you live free and unashamed.

CHAPTER 22

The Keys

Grace unlocks truth.

When we started our church in New Mexico the tagline we chose was, "It's all about Jesus, from Genesis to Revelation." We chose it to emphasize that Jesus is the center of everything in the Bible and should be the center of all we do.

Another thing we emphasized in our little church was that no one should take what is preached and just accept it. The Scripture is very clear that no one stands between you and God. You don't have to have a teacher. You can go to God and His Word and hear from Him directly. Does that mean we shouldn't have Biblical teachers? I don't think God intended that to be so since He says that He makes some of us teachers. But it does mean that you don't *need* a teacher to know the truth. If you do have one, always scrutinize what they say by holding it up to the truth of God's Word. And that goes for *Radical Grace* too! Check my assertions against the text of the Bible. You can look up all the references that are listed the Appendix in the back of this book. It is up to you to confirm what you read and hear so you are not led astray.

Some people have told me it is hard to read the Bible and understand it. I know that some passages take some undivided attention, study, and research to grasp. Especially some of what the prophets say that seems vague and mysterious. But you don't need to start there. Instead, start with the New Testament, and utilize the "keys" that I am going to teach you so you can unlock the treasure of God's Word and find His radical grace within its pages!

Not all Bible studies or things we read on the internet are in line with Biblical truth. Let's be honest, even scripture can be used out of context to make a desired point. We must be careful not to accept a lesson as truth just because it includes a verse or two from the Bible. If a person applies scripture in the wrong context, we can be misguided and drawn away from the truth.

In this chapter I hope to equip you to defend against the influence of false teaching. I will take you through the process of identifying false doctrine. Following is an example of a subtly legalistic usage of scripture that I witnessed not long ago. You will see how applying certain keys help to unlock the truth and to avoid graceless doctrine.

During the Covid-19 lockdown of 2020, I saw a post on social media that quoted 2 Chronicles 7:14 from the Old Testament. I'm sure the people who shared it were desperate for the virus to vanish and for people to be safe, and in their desperation, they failed to see that this passage, when misused, preaches a legalistic approach to God.

> *"If My people who are called by My name will humble themselves, and pray and seek My face, and turn from their wicked ways, then I will hear from heaven, and will forgive their sin and heal their land."* (2 Ch 7:14)

You may not immediately see that this is a misleading message, but if you look carefully, you will see that it preaches a legalistic approach to God and leaves out Jesus and His grace altogether. Note each key that I used to unlock the truth as I take you through my study of this verse.

Context. First, let's consider the context. Contextual clues will shed light on this passage's meaning and help us see the truth.

The LORD was talking to Solomon and the Jewish nation when He spoke this verse in 2 Chronicles. This Old Testament passage was meant for a specific leader, for a specific audience, and for a specific time. That context matters.

This verse isn't a formula that over the millennia people were to apply to get God to act in their various situations. We tend to make formulas out of scriptures, especially when we feel helpless and just want answers. But God is Spirit, and there is no formula as to how He works. We must be careful not to assume that our current situation fits perfectly within the context of what was going on in the lives of the people in the Bible.

Much of the scripture is not so specific to a group of people or to a particular era and can be beautifully encouraging and helpful in our lives. We need to discern if any scripture we are using or reading is correctly applied not only within the context of the audience and era, but also in the context of Jesus, the New Covenant, grace, faith, our new nature, and the mission of the Holy Spirit. Taking care to note the context of what we read, share, and hear will help us steer clear of the incorrect application of scripture.

Law/CODE. Next, this verse is an "if-then" statement from the Old Testament. Recall that "if-then" statements are a red flag; they are usually devoid of Jesus and grace because they condition God's actions on our obedience.

The implication is that if "those called by My name" (Christians) do *not* do what the verse asks, then He won't answer our prayers for our loved ones, our nation, and our world. Do you see the problem with that? The logic really breaks down when you consider how it might work in practice. Just how many Christians need to do this? And how well? Will He answer if just 10% of us obey? Or does it have to be 50%, 75%, or 100%? What, exactly, do we need to do for God to fulfill His "then" part? There is no way to answer this if we put this rule on ourselves.

Because of our familiarity with the work/reward system, these types of teachings easily sneak past us.

When used in a New Covenant context, this verse from 2 Chronicles is legalistic and works-based. It is not grounded in grace.

Dual Nature. Because the concept of our dual natures is not very widely taught, much of what we consume as followers of Christ doesn't distinguish that we are now born anew spiritually and we now approach God spiritually, not in our flesh. This verse in 2 Chronicles suggests that believers must accomplish a list of to-dos before God forgives them, hears their prayers, and heals their land. If you are in Christ, you have already humbled yourself, you already pray, you already seek His face, you have turned from your flesh and have been reborn in the spirit. You are already forgiven. In Jesus, our new nature is already separated from the old man or woman of wicked ways. That part of us still exists, but it isn't who we identify as now. And in that new identity, God is right by our side, ready and willing to hear our prayers and answer them according to His will.

Covenants. Jesus and what He did for us are missing when we apply this Old Covenant verse from 2 Chronicles to a New Covenant situation. Jesus ushered in the New Covenant which created an "I will" relationship between God and His children, and the One doing everything is God. We don't have to fulfill a list of good deeds to pray to God and ask Him to heal people of a virus. He receives us as we are. While we were sinners, Christ died for us. He accepts us as we are, broken in our flesh yet healed in our spirit. He hears our prayers without us having to uphold some standard of moral obedience because He has already made us righteous. The New Covenant is a covenant of grace.

Sanctification/Righteousness. As New Covenant believers, we don't have the same deal as the Jewish nation. As partakers of the New Covenant, we have an individual relationship with our God. In the Old Testament, people relied on their fellow citizens to obey God's commands for their nation to be blessed or not cursed. They couldn't approach God directly. They had to go through the priests; we do not. Because Jesus made us righteous and holy, we can go to God at any moment with any prayer. We do not need to clean up our flesh or go through an extensive ceremonial cleansing to approach Him. Jesus already cleaned us up.

Jesus/Grace. Jesus became the new High Priest and Mediator of this new deal. Jesus is the only person between you and the Father. Once you have put your faith in Jesus, you can go to Him anywhere, anytime, without having to do anything.

We have direct access to the Father through Jesus even though we still have a sinful nature. We don't need to hope some portion of the children of God turn from their sin for God to hear our prayers, heal us, or forgive our sins. We have a personal, intimate relationship with God.

Using the 2 Chronicles verse in a New Covenant context is confusing and is the opposite of grace because it requires the "work" of turning from sin. In Christ, we don't have this "work" requirement. We may simply go boldly to His throne because we have faith in Jesus. Simply talk to God about what is on your heart.

Again, I know the people who shared that post did not intend to preach a legalistic approach to God. The sad thing is that too often, grace is not being adequately taught, and therefore, it is easily lost in the doctrine that Christ-followers often "preach." And regrettably, such a post suggests to people that they are separated from God because of their sin, or other people's sins, and they cannot approach Him unless they clean themselves up first and everyone else does as well.

Let's look at a richer description of the keys I use to unlock any passage or teaching that I hear or read. We will examine each one of the keys so you can use them to unlock the Gospel of Grace, the truth of the Word, and any doctrine you encounter.

Key 1 – Context

When you are reading your Bible, noting the context of any passage helps you interpret scripture correctly. Whenever you come to a verse with a meaning that you're unsure of, make sure to understand the context of the book, its author, its intended audience, and the context within that part of the chapter. For example, Paul won't shift from talking about being free from the law in one sentence to saying you must obey the law to please God in the next. If such a discrepancy appears, "zoom" out and read the verses that precede and follow the sentence in question (or perhaps read the whole chapter) to gain a better sense of what the author is communicating. Studying in context, and not just looking at scriptures in isolation from the surrounding text, will help you better understand the Bible.

Key 2 – Covenants

You are not a member of the Old Covenant; rather, you are a member of the New Covenant. You are not in an "if-then" relationship with God but an "I will" relationship. You do not have to go through anyone other than Jesus. You can go boldly to the throne of grace and approach God directly through Him, the Mediator of the New Covenant.

This key is crucial to rightly dividing the Word of God. When Old Covenant scripture is preached to New Covenant believers, there is a risk of creating a legalistic message. Jesus changed the way we approach God through His bringing in the New Covenant.

There is another covenant key issue that I have often come across that we must be careful to note. Teachings or sayings that attempt to combine Old and New Covenant doctrine create a mixed message and is usually incredibly confusing. We must distinguish the differences between the covenants and consider the interpretation of doctrine based on those differences.

Key 3 – Law/CODE

John, Luke, and Paul have all explained that you are no longer under the law but under grace. The law was to make sin abound and to reveal to the world that everyone needs a Savior. If a teaching demands you fulfill the Mosaic law or any form of the CODE, then it is false. Jesus already fulfilled the law for you and, therefore, freed you from the bondage of the law and obedience for righteousness.

Key 4 – Dual Nature

You have a two-part nature. We can see this as a recurring theme in Paul's writings, especially when he talks about putting off the old man and putting on the new and walking in the newness of life. Jesus Himself said you must be born of water and the Spirit. In Romans chapter 7, Paul narrates his struggle with the sin that resides in him and that the real *him* desires to act differently.

Your two-part nature resolves the seemingly confusing situation you find yourself in; you are a new creation in Christ, yet you still have temptations. Your spirit is at odds with your flesh. Even though we drag around our old sinful self, our identity is our newly-born-in-the-Spirit self. Any message that doesn't separate your flesh from your new spirit will most likely lead to a preoccupation with sin and works, which causes self-righteousness, pride, and judgment, or frustration, shame, and doubt.

Key 5 – Sanctification/Righteousness

You have been both justified, which declares you innocent and makes you righteous, and sanctified, declaring you separated to serve God and made holy. These are gifts of God, by His grace, through your faith in Jesus. Sadly, many doctrines misguide us about our holiness and righteousness. I understand why. These truths are difficult to believe because we still have a sinful nature. That is why understanding your two different natures is so important. The Bible is very clear that Jesus did these things for you. You are equipped to do whatever God asks you to do. You are already there. There is no need to work to get to some level of right-eousness before sharing your talents, gifts, and love with the world. Walking in righteousness, in the Spirit, is possible for the new you!

Any teaching that tells you that you must work on becoming a better person or more like Jesus is ignorant of the fact that you are already justified and sanctified. It is based on works, not grace.

Key 6 – Spirit

Another key is making sure the Spirit is present and properly addressed. I have experienced many teachings that over-emphasize one ministry of the Spirit while ignoring the others. I have also experienced teachings that don't even mention the Spirit. It is important to know Who the Spirit is, what His mission is, and that He is living inside of you. He helps you, guides you, pro-duces fruit in you, and intercedes for you with the

Father. Surrender your life to Him, let Him lead you as you walk in Him, and you will see the incredible blessing it is to see Him work in your life and the lives of those around you.

Beware of teachings that either ignore the Spirit or overemphasize one of His ministries over the others. His mission in our lives is one of the most significant aspects of our new relationship with God as He ministers to us in many ways.

Key 7 – Jesus/Grace

At the very beginning of this book, I told you one of the keys to rightly dividing the Word of God was to keep in mind the big picture, that the Bible is all about Jesus. I am putting grace and Jesus together as a key because everything Jesus did for you was established in the grace of the Father. Anything you read or listen to must be foundationally rooted in Jesus or His radical grace, or it isn't a New Covenant doctrine or the true Gospel. If you want to know if a statement or teaching is true to the Gospel, just put Jesus or grace in the middle of it. If any doctrine can stand on its own, without Jesus or God's grace, there is a good chance it is contrary to the Word of God.

Let's look at a few examples of familiar things we hear, contrasted with the truth. Words that reference keys are bolded and italicized.

We hear: Christians must not rest nor become complacent in the battle against sin.

The truth: It is not our job to battle our sin. If it is, what good is *Jesus*? He conquered our sin, ***He died for our sin***, He forgave our sin, He busted the chains that sin had on us, He made us *holy* and *righteous*, He gave us a *new nature*, and He gave us the power of His *Spirit* living in us. The battle has been won. Where there is no *law*, sin is not imputed. We can rest in Him. The Gospel of Grace is not about battling our sin, it is about living the new life that Jesus has given us. Our new life in Christ isn't about sin; it is about love.

Keys: 2, 3, 4, 5, 6, 7

We hear: Practice spiritual discipline (Read your Bible, pray, worship, serve) and examine how you have indulged sin, then compare that to your pursuit of righteousness.

The truth: This is all about you and your efforts, not about God's *grace* of the *New Covenant*. The word *discipline* invokes an adherence to the **CODE**. Doing these acts for the sake of becoming righteous is what Paul calls works. *Jesus* already gave you His *righteousness* when you were *born again*. We read the Bible, pray, worship, serve, and love others not as a responsibility but as a response to His radical grace and leading of His *Spirit* living in us.

Keys: 2, 3, 4, 5, 6, 7

We hear: Jesus has forgiven you, so too, you should forgive others.

The truth: This is true and possible! And we can confirm its validity through the keys. I shared with you my journey of forgiving my abusers in a previous chapter, but I'd like to share with you the specific keys that I applied to that process. We can read many scriptures in the New Testament about forgiving others. The scriptures found in the New Testament that speak to followers of Christ are speaking to *New Covenant* believers. The *law* taught me that I have been born unrighteous, and that in my flesh, I am not more righteous than my offenders, so I refuse to judge them by their flesh. However, I have been born again with a *dual nature*, so I *can* choose love because I have been made new, *righteous*, and *holy* and have the fruit of the *Spirit* available to me. I can walk in my flesh and stay angry or walk in the Spirit and live out love. I chose love. The only way I can choose love is because of *Jesus* and the fact that He has blessed me with these gifts. I could not have forgiven my abusers without those gifts of *grace*.

Keys: 2, 3, 4, 5, 6, 7

Here are some simple questions to ask of anything you read and hear to ensure that it is truth.

1. Can it stand on its own without Jesus? If so, it's not the Gospel.
2. Is it about you fixing your fleshly nature? If so, it

is about a futile pursuit, not walking freely according to the Spirit.

3. Does it include a condition for you or an "if-then" requirement to receive a reaction, blessing, or answer from God? Then most likely it is Old Covenant or based on works, not based in grace or the New Covenant.

4. Is it in disagreement with the context of the scripture in which it is found, or with the Biblical message of the Gospel of Grace in general? Then it probably isn't true or from God.

5. Is it void of the Spirit of God? If so, it can't be spiritually focused and lacks the availability of the power of the Spirit to work in your life.

6. Does it require you to obey the Mosaic Law or the CODE? If so, it excludes Jesus, His fulfillment of the law, and His nailing the law and any written requirements to the cross. It is about works, not grace.

7. Does it require you to participate in your sanctification? If so, it omits God's gracious act of making you holy through Jesus' sacrifice once for all.

Simply place Jesus and grace in the middle of anything you hear or read, and you will unlock the genuine Gospel of Grace and avoid being seduced by false teaching.

I have mentioned some Biblical warnings already, but did you know that Jesus specifically warned us not to be caught up in legalistic teachings? He cautioned against the teachings of the Pharisees and Sadducees because He knew the risk of us being led astray by legalism. Both the Pharisees and Sadducees were all about the Jewish law. They were steeped in the law. So much so that they added extra rules to the ones God had already given them. They were the CODE before the CODE was cool! Many of them couldn't accept that Jesus' grace was real and that He was who He said He was. As a result, they rejected their own Messiah.

That desire for legalism didn't end with the resurrection. In his letter to the people of Colosse, Paul warns that we should not be cheated out of our new life and freedom in Christ by man's traditions and teachings. Those traditions are conceived according to the principles of this world, the fleshly, physical world, not the heavenly, spiritual world, of which we are now citizens. They are teachings that are not Biblical and deny God's radical grace.

This mental and spiritual battle has been waged against the followers of Christ since the day Jesus ascended into eternity and took a seat next to the Father. The devil thought he won at the cross, but because he didn't, he conceived a new battle plan. His plan is to pull God's children away from the freedom and grace that he knows Jesus has given us. The enemy tries to keep us entrenched in the battle against our sin, in bondage to laws and rules, and shackled to shame. It is time to break free, my friend!

I hope and pray these seven keys will help you to

---

unlock anything you hear or read so you are not led away from the truth of the Gospel of Grace or put into bondage of obedience to the CODE. Once I understood these seven keys, they unlocked the meaning of passages I had struggled to understand. They can do the same for you. Use them and allow radical grace to unlock the truth for you.

CHAPTER 23

The Throne

Grace enables intimacy with God.

"Where are you?" God asked.

God's question was simple. This loving question teaches us about our relationship with Him.

In Chapter 4, I talked about Adam and Eve being tempted to eat the forbidden fruit. The fruit was beautiful and looked tasty. Eve couldn't resist the idea of becoming wise if she ate the luscious fruit. As we know, she bit into it and offered it to Adam as well. Immediately they realized they were naked. Shame made them feel exposed. Their instinct was to cover themselves with fig leaves and try to hide from God. In their panic, they took cover among the trees and bushes.

This hits a little close to home. Many times, in my life, I wished there was a garden or underground bunker I could hide in.

Later, God walked in the garden. What was the first thing He said to them?

He didn't say, "Adam, Eve, get your disobedient leaf-covered selves out here right now and tell Me what on earth you have done!"

Instead, He asked, "Where are you?"

God knew what had happened. He *is* God, after all. I submit that He wanted Adam and Eve to face their fears and realize they didn't need to hide from Him. He wanted them to come to Him, not go into hiding. He had the answer to Adam and Eve's problem. He not only covered them at that time with animal skins so they wouldn't feel ashamed, but He also had a plan in store to solve the problem that all of humanity was now facing. He wanted them to allow Him to love them.

I had to realize that God had the answer to my shame as well. It fascinates me that I took on shame from something someone else did to me. This is a common experience, internalizing the shame that our offenders should feel. I tried for years to cover my shame by my own efforts, but to no avail. I wasn't running to God with my problem, I was hiding from Him. Or so I thought. Once I learned that God wants us to come to Him, right into His presence, with faith that He heals and forgives, I didn't just wander over, I ran.

God wants us to run toward Him, even when – and especially when – we do things that we are ashamed of. The heart of God is for us, not against us. He wants fellowship with us. He desires and longs to be in our lives. Yes, Adam and Eve created a separation between humanity and God through their disobedience. That separation is necessary between a holy God and unright-eous people. But God doesn't want us to hide in the shadows. That is why He sent Jesus. Jesus was sent to make a path out of the shame and into His arms.

In this chapter, we will explore a topic at the very core of this issue: the Throne of God. Since Adam and Eve were evicted from Eden, people were not allowed to approach God as easily as they had it in the garden. But thanks to Jesus, we have a whole new gig. God made it possible for us to be with Him and not hide from Him any longer.

In the Old Testament, we learn about the tabernacle of God. This sacred place was where God came to talk to the nation of Israel. Really, we have it great now. Back then, it was difficult – terrifying, even – to commune with God.

Maybe you have read about this in the Book of Exodus. Picture a room behind a big thick curtain. In that room, called the Most Holy Place, God came and met with the high priest.

Behind that big curtain sat the Ark of the Testimony. It was a large box overlaid with gold and topped with a pure gold lid called the mercy seat, which was flanked by two angel-like figures called cherubim. God spoke from above the mercy seat between the two angel-like statues.

Man, or priests, could not enter just any ol' time into that Most Holy Place. When it was time for the priest to enter past the veil, into the presence of the LORD, he had to go through an extensive ceremonial consecration. God required the priest to obey Him precisely because He required perfection, righteousness, and obedience. And the general population could never enter His presence because God is holy, and they were not.

That was how it was done in the Old Covenant. Only the priest could communicate with God and could do so only after he went through the meticulous cleansing ritual. The regular folks didn't get to approach the LORD.

But we are participants of the New Covenant where Jesus is the High Priest, and He changed the way we approach God.

Scripture tells us when Jesus died on the cross, the veil in the temple was torn in two. That event was symbolic in that Christ's redemption brings us through the barrier, into intimacy with God, and into His presence. We have fellowship with Him through our relationship with Jesus.

The veil that tore in the earthly temple represented the heavenly veil of Jesus' flesh, or body, given on the cross. Because of His sacrifice, we may go fearlessly into the presence of God by the blood of Jesus. And we can go without shame. We can go with the full assurance of faith. This, my friend, is something so amazing I cannot even think of a word to describe it. Because of what Jesus did, we can enter the presence of God. And we can go with confidence to the God of the universe who loves us dearly. He won't turn us away or shun us in shame as we spend time in His presence because we have been washed and made righteous.

Not only can we approach God in person now, but we can go *boldly* to Him. Going boldly means we can go with our heads held high, through the tear in the big curtain, and talk to God about anything. That means we can enter His presence in confidence, knowing He loves us, He digs us, and nothing we say is going to surprise Him. We can talk about anything without worrying that somehow, we will lose our place in Him, be ignored, or be condemned. We can stand firmly in His grace and mercy.

We can talk to God when we need help. We receive God's mercy for our mistakes and God's grace that helps us when we need it.

As we boldly approach God, we should understand He will not be shocked if we talk to Him about something we think will disappoint Him. He does love it when we walk in righteousness, but, as I have explained, we still have our flesh, and we are all addicted to sin in our fleshly nature to some degree. That is no surprise to Him. He knows. That is why Jesus had to do what He did to allow us to be able to come out of the bushes and connect with Him.

God wants us to come to Him and tell Him our struggles. He can help us figure out why we are struggling to choose our spirit instead of our flesh. We can ask Him and seek His strength in times of weakness and choose the way to escape temptation. He can help when we feel like we must please our flesh to be satisfied.

As I have mentioned, everyone struggles to one degree or another with their flesh. Those struggles can be a reaction to something that has happened in our past which drives us to protect ourselves. Other struggles may have made us feel a need to fulfill something that is missing in our lives. Everyone has dealt with hardship, disappointment, sadness, neglect, or injustice. For some, it doesn't weigh them down very much. They can leave it at the cross and move on. For others, though, this is a more difficult task. God wants so desperately for us to come boldly to Him, cry out to Him, talk to Him directly and share our deepest secrets and emotions. We can ask Him to reveal to us and heal us from whatever is causing us to harm ourselves or others by way of our sinful flesh. Know that your relationship is based in grace and His desire is for you to come to Him and receive it!

Even if your life isn't defined by struggle, you might feel like you are merely going through the motions of life or feel unsatisfied. Talk to God. Ask Him to fill you up with His grace and to give you direction in what His calling is for your life. Maybe you are already thinking about what God is calling you to do. If this is true, make sure the feeling you must do something does not stem from a misplaced sense of guilt. That's not coming from the throne of grace. Perhaps a person (you, or someone else) is instilling you with that guilt needlessly. On the other hand, if that calling is a desire God put on your heart, then go to His throne and ask Him what He wants you to do next. God will lead you to inspiration. Go, follow Him, step out in faith. Watch what you and He can do together when you work as a team.

Because of your new nature, even if you are struggling in the flesh, in your spirit you can approach God and ask Him to guide you. Ask Him to show you how to use what you are passionate about for good in this world. You don't have to work in a ministry or go on a mission to "do more for God." Those things are wonderful ways to serve God but are only for those called to do them. You may be called to coach kids' sports, visit nursing homes, or play your guitar and sing songs on the street to put smiles on faces. Or you might minister to that one child of yours for 20 years because that is all the energy and time you have. There is no one answer. There are billions of ways God will have His children walk in righteousness and do good works. My friend, the answer might simply be to love others in whatever you do.

You might need to enter through the veil on behalf of a loved one or yourself for healing a physical injury, illness, or emotional difficulty. Or you may seek God about raising your children, finding answers for your marriage, or obtaining solutions for a problem at work. No matter what it is that you need, you can go boldly and confidently to God, knowing that God is for you, not against you. He knows all your failures and accepts and loves you anyway. He *wants* an intimate, personal relationship with you. Go boldly beyond that torn veil. Get out from under that bush and answer His question, "Where are you?" with, "Here I am!"

I'll be in the throne room talking to God. See you there!

CHAPTER 24

The Moment

Grace exists in the moment.

My dear friend, Deanna, shared a wonderful perspective with me once. She noted that when facing something fearful in our future, if we dwell on worry *before* we are in the midst of it, we are living through it in our minds over and over without God's grace. But once we are actually going through whatever it is, we have the benefit of God's grace in those moments.

She is right! Grace exists in the now.

Living in the moment is living where God meets us. God is the creator of time and knows our past and our future, but He chooses to be with us right now, in this moment.

In the last chapter we explored the truth that we can approach His throne any time day or night because He has made us righteous. But it is also true that because we are His children, He meets us where we are. We not only get to go to His house, but He comes to ours as well!

Because we live on this planet, and we must deal with difficult things, there are times when we are weak and need to rely on His strength. The Bible tells us that Jesus' grace is sufficient for us and that when we don't think we can handle something, His strength is perfect, and He offers to hold us up. It is amazing what we can endure because in those times, He is our strength.

One particularly trying time for us was when our youngest daughter was diagnosed with cancer in her leg. God brought us to a surgeon who removed it, and, praise God, she is cancer-free now. Along the way, my husband and I grew closer to our daughter. We prayed together, spent more time together, and were there for each other on the hard days.

We simplify such stories when we tell others because none of us has the time to hear the whole tale, or we think so, anyway.

But that description doesn't adequately explain our *actual* experience. It would take me weeks to write to you about what we did every moment to get from the beginning to the end of the ordeal. I would have to describe every moment to you for you to grasp it completely; all the prayer, surgeries, emotions, driving to and from hospitals and doctors' offices, rainstorms we endured, cars we borrowed, bandages, disappointments, setbacks, smells and sadness, hope, and encouragements, financial commitments, and on and on. You might be interested in the story, but you probably would start nodding off. To God though, this time in our lives was important and He showed up. He was there every moment.

All we could do was live in the present moment and

get through it with God. And it was God in those moments, one after another, that got us through to the end. I needed to trust God when I heard the news and started having a panic attack. It was trusting Him as I dressed the gaping hole in her leg twice a day as tears seeped from my eyes. And it was trusting Him that as we kept going, moment by moment, He was with us, and His plan was in action. All we had was God in every single moment. We just faithfully did the little things every day, moment by moment.

We couldn't wallow in the pain of the past, or regret that we hadn't brought her to a doctor sooner. We couldn't focus on the fear of the future because that would have immobilized us from doing what we needed to do each day. And in those moments, God came to *our* house.

In hindsight, we can look back at what His plan was for us during that experience. We can see how He orchestrated the discovery of the tumor to begin with. How a move across the country saved our daughter's life. How the time together brought healing to our relationships through the trust and love that we had to share with each other every day. Those moments, good or bad, brought us to the end of that chapter in our story.

In each moment of that journey, the grace of God comforted us and gave us hope.

He could have said to us, "Ok, now you are my child, I'll catch you later. See you in the end when you come to My house."

But He didn't. He said He would be with us and never leave us. He would come to us and live with us so He could be there every moment of every day. No matter what kind of day we are having, He is there to comfort us in the difficult moments and to rejoice, laugh, and smile with us in the great ones. And no matter what is going on in our lives, we can always be thankful and worship Him because in those moments His grace is fresh and lives in real time.

We all understand what it means to live in the moment, and we see the value in it, but we don't always do it, do we? Too often, we are focused on the future and what's next, or looking back at our failures, wallowing in our shame, depressed. We miss being present in the now.

We can, of course, relish our past successes, learn from our mistakes, and look forward in hope. But why do we waste our present by squandering our attention somewhere else in time? We can't change the past, and we don't know if we even have tomorrow. That sounds a little gloomy, but it is true. Only God knows the number of our days.

One thing that robs us of our moment is progressive sanctification. It keeps us living in the past or the future and it steals the now. If we are supposed to be progressing in our holiness, how can we help but look back to compare where we've been with where we are presently? Or we look to our future and hope we do better, or at least hope we don't do worse. If we live by progressive sanctification, we never know where we stand in Christ and we live each moment in worrying about failure. Moments filled with fear. Moments wasted.

Radical grace, though, gives us a better way. Instead of living in comparison to our past or panic about our future, we may rest in knowing we are already made holy. We have been equipped with everything we need to walk in the righteousness that Jesus has imputed to us. We have the Spirit that offers His divine power to our spirit, so we may use our moments for walking in the holiness we already have been given through our sanctification.

Another thing that steals our moments is trying to obey the Mosaic Law or the CODE. Jesus made it very clear that He has taken the law out of our way, and it is no longer our master. We can't fulfill it anyway. And manmade rules keep us focused on obedience to them rather than love toward others. Moments spent focused on an impossible to-do list makes us disenchanted and exhausted. Moments filled with frustration. Moments wasted.

Radical grace is different. God's grace does not require us to strive for obedience. We can rejoice in doing the one thing Jesus asks us to do, which is to love others. But don't approach it as a single-item to-do list in your flesh. Flip on the light switch, walk in your new man or woman, and love others beyond the checklist of dos and don'ts. Each moment of your day can be lived in the love and peace of Jesus as you lay down the burden of obedience to the CODE.

Focusing on our past sins is another moment-stealer as it afflicts us with hopelessness. Continually looking into the rearview mirror not only distracts us from doing what we can do in Christ, but it drags us down into a pit of regret. Those moments direct our attention toward needless shame, for which Jesus died. Moments of despair. Moments wasted.

Radical grace keeps our sin from stealing those moments. We can cherish the present without fixating on the past. Christ gave Himself so we wouldn't have to be held back by or brought to a halt by our sin. We can trust that He did, indeed, forgive us of those things, stand up in faith, and start using our moments as the new child of God that we are. Each day we are given new moments to make great.

Because of God's radical grace and our ability to use all the spiritual blessings that He has given us, we are able to use our moments for amazing things. Let's not waste them on things He already took care of for us.

You are probably familiar with the verse in Psalms that tells us that today is the day that God made, and we should rejoice. Some days are hard for us to rejoice and be glad. But God knows about today. After all, the Bible says He made it. He knows the days we hear bad news or are facing a great trial. God tells us through Jeremiah that

He has a plan of peace and hope for us, and He wants to give us a future. He works all things together for good and Jesus told us His yoke is easy and His burden is light.

How can all this be? How can we rejoice when we are going through something hard? Because of His radical grace, we can have pure unfettered faith that He is with us in those moments and has a plan for them. His grace exists in that moment for us to seize and trust that our loving God is with us. When we don't see the answers and start to walk in fear, we can grasp His hand and say, "Daddy, please hold me up today. Be my strength. Be with me in this moment."

And He will wrap His arms around us and hold us tight.

My friend, we can press on. Like Paul says in Philippians, we can forget those things that are behind us and reach forward as we cherish and trust God in every moment. And as we walk in that faith and draw from His Spirit to love others, we will be creating moments that have spiritual and eternal value.

Grace followed us during the difficult chapter we endured with our daughter's cancer diagnosis. From the waiting room of the doctor's office and the daily bandaging of her leg to the day she was declared cancer free, God came to us, and we are so very thankful for His grace in those moments.

All we can do is live in the moment because that is all we have, but it is also all we need because that is where we find God and His grace. When we reach the end of our life's journey, and we are standing in His presence looking back at our lives, God will tell us we did well, and we were faithful servants. Grace isn't only given when we ask Jesus to forgive us for our sins, it endures throughout our lives and into the moment we stand in glory. And in that moment, it will be evident that His grace is truly radical.

CHAPTER 25

The Victory

Grace gives us the victory.

Pretzel, Polly Perfect, Laurie, Laurel, Aunt Yo-Yo, Honey, Mom, and LaLa are all names I have been called by various people throughout my life. Most of these nicknames make sense. I was called Pretzel when I was 4 years old because I was an acrobatic dancer and very flexible – I could literally bend myself in half either forward or backward. My nephew called me Aunt Yo-Yo when he was little as he couldn't pronounce Laurel. It was endearing. I was – *am*, really – a little yoyo, so I can relate to that name too. I'm Honey to my husband, Mom to my children and LaLa to my grandbabies. Those are names I hear most often and speak well to who I am. But the one name in the list that I no longer relate to and that used to upset me is Polly Perfect.

When I was young, my mother would call me "Polly Perfect." It wasn't flattery; on the contrary, it was derogatory, and I sensed that. When she called me Polly I usually spun into a whirlwind of frustration and anger. I would go into my room, plop onto my bed, and just cry. Truthfully, I hit the pillow and screamed into it in addition to the crying. She believed that I thought I was perfect. Nothing could be further from the truth, which is why it so frustrated me.

Now that I'm grown and have gone through years of healing and self-reflection, I understand the situation better. To my family I probably came across as self-righteous and judgmental in my efforts as a perfectionist. What they didn't know, though, was *why* I was being Polly Perfect.

As I have previously described, I felt pressured to be perfect on the outside because I felt so damaged on the inside. I needed to try my best to do good at everything I did so I could feel ok and accepted. Mom didn't realize that she was adding to my feelings of worthlessness when she called me that name. I don't hold any of that against her. I know she was just trying to get through life and what this world threw at her. She couldn't have known what my thoughts and feelings were. She never asked, and I never told her.

Mom stopped calling me Polly once I was a bit older, but I came to realize later in life that I *was* being a Polly Perfect both back then and into my adult years. I was striving to be perfect in my flesh. I wasn't Laurel, I was Polly, and I needed to discover who I really was.

As I grew in my understanding of God's radical grace, I started to see Polly fade away. As I accepted God's love and learned about forgiveness, mercy, and the blessings Jesus has given me, someone started to emerge that I hadn't ever met before. Her name is Laurel.

Originally, my parents were going to name me Noël

since I was due on Christmas. Noël means *born on Christmas day*. However, Mom's doctor didn't want to be delivering babies on Christmas, so he induced her labor, and I was born a few days earlier. So, I'm not Noël, I'm Laurel.

My namesake was my great-uncle, Laurel Wilson Splittgerber. If that isn't a German name, what is? He was born in 1918 and died a couple years before I was born. My parents wanted to name me in his honor, so I was *named* Laurel.

Laurel is who I had been looking for my entire life. I finally discovered her and became authentically Laurel when I found victory in Jesus through His radical grace. That's how I *became* Laurel.

By the way, the name Laurel means *victory*.

Victory evokes many synonyms: success, triumph, conquest, win. We desire victory in sports, our careers, and war. Our history on planet earth is filled with stories of victory and defeat, but the greatest victory ever won is the victory Jesus had through His death and resurrection. He is the ultimate victor, the One who has overcome and achieved success in His mission to bring salvation to the world.

Jesus' death and resurrection defeated sin's control and death itself. He has overcome the enemy, Satan, and He offers to share His spoils with the world. He has brought us out of darkness and into Him, the Light, and has given us a new life in Him. Amazingly, He invites us to participate in His victory.

In that victory, Jesus offers us some priceless treasure! For example, we are encouraged in the Book of John when Jesus tells us to be of good cheer. The word *cheer* in that verse means to have *courage* or *comfort*. We can be courageous and comforted by the fact that Jesus has overcome the world.

The Bible tells us that God, who is in us, is greater than the enemy who is in the world. This truth helps us see that we need not fear anything the devil throws at us. We are also told that we are capable of walking in the spiritual kingdom rather than this worldly one because we have been born into His kingdom. We can be courageous and comforted by these truths.

Even when we feel like everything is pushing in on us, or we are overwhelmed by our circumstances, we need not despair. In fact, we can do the opposite. We can find comfort in the One who conquered it all. And when life feels like a battle, we will not be destroyed, but we can be courageous knowing that Jesus went to battle for us and has already won the war. He is our strength and our refuge through every storm. There is nothing we can't do in Him. Because He has overcome the world, we benefit. By faith in Him, we have overcome the world as well. Because of all these blessings Jesus has given us, we are victorious in Him.

If you poke around the internet, you will find many commentaries that discuss victory in Jesus. However, it is rare to find one that ties that victory to God's grace rather than our own works. Many blogs and online articles about living a victorious life fall short of true victory because they lay burdensome baggage on the reader.

First the author will say Jesus gives us our victory through faith in Him, which is true. But then many go on to say that to have a victorious life we need to avoid sin, or *do* this, or *don't do* that. I have read articles that say if you feel you are not victorious and have drifted away from God, you should read your Bible more, hang around Christians instead of unsaved people, or don't spend so much time focused on your career or hobbies. Others say we are to pursue holiness and stay in the fight, persevere. Those suggestions don't sound like a victory or a win to me, they sound like the battle.

Which is it? Did Jesus give us victory or are we to obtain it on our own? We are victorious in Christ. He did the battling for us, and He has already won. It's over.

I submit to you that this is the type of teaching that causes people to feel defeated in the first place. So, people write more articles about how to live a victorious life. They see the issue but don't pause to look deeper into why it persists.

My dear friend, please don't fall for the lie that victory is only won by your own efforts. Victory is given to you freely because of your faith in Jesus. That's it.

Grace that frees you from shame and offers you freedom to be you, is the victory Jesus offers. It is a radical kind of grace.

What does it mean to have a victorious life? A life of victory is a life that demonstrates freedom, fulfillment and meaning. We have freedom to rest from trying to become someone that God has already made us to be. Victory in Him means that we are holy and righteous and freed from the control of sin. Freedom is knowing we don't have to live up to a moral standard that we simply cannot accomplish. Because of our victory in Christ, we are free to explore the limitless possibilities of living a life that is triumphant.

A life of victory is a life of fulfillment as we soak in every moment of our lives, love those whom we encounter, and have daily chats with the Creator of the universe. Our joy is full, and we go about our lives with a strong, underlying peace no matter what happens. We can trust that God is with us when we pursue the things that bring us satisfaction and happiness. Not the kind of satisfaction that we get from a fleeting fleshly moment, but the kind of deep satisfaction that only comes when we are resonating with God in what we do in our spirit.

We also cultivate lives that have meaning and purpose, with one main goal at heart: to love through giving ourselves to others. Jesus modeled this very well for us when He washed the disciples' feet. We too, find purpose and meaning in serving those around us. And when we do, we are creating eternal value. There are a million different ways we can offer ourselves to others because

God has made each of us unique.

What are your talents and gifts that God has given you so you can serve and love the world around you? Are you saving lives in a hospital, running a restaurant, staying home raising children, or sweeping the streets? Whatever you do in a day, you matter, and what you are doing has purpose for you, your family, and your world.

We don't need to feel pressured to accomplish some great thing for God every day, or think we need to build something big for Him in our lifetime. If we love Him and love others deeply in the moments we have with them, we will be doing exactly what we have been created to do. God uses us in different ways. Some of us will affect thousands of people, while others of us will touch the lives of a few. But every person that we encounter is important to Jesus and we get to encourage, support, and speak hope into their lives when we interact with them.

I have found the life I am talking about. His victory has become my victory. I am no longer bound by depression, obsessive compulsive disorder, agoraphobia, and self-destruction. The reason I no longer suffer these things is because I have embraced His radical grace for myself, and I won't let go. Because of the freedom and fulfillment Jesus' victory has afforded me, I can be myself. I am both my flesh and my new spirit, but I view my flesh differently now. I own up to it but am no longer overwhelmed by shame because of it. I don't have to hide who I am from God, nor from you.

And neither do you.

My friend, you are a victorious child of God. Embrace that victorious life that Jesus has for you. You are an overcomer in Jesus. You are righteous and whole, forgiven, and free to live victoriously thanks to God's incredible radical grace.

CHAPTER 26

The End, Or Is It the Beginning?

Embrace God's radical grace.

Are you excited? I sure am. Now that we have come to the end of *Radical Grace: Live Free and Unashamed* I am just as excited as I was to share my thoughts with you at the start. I am excited because I realize that you are really at a beginning. Your new life in God's radical grace begins now!

Together we have explored a great deal of territory. We started at the beginning of time checking in on the lives of Adam and Eve. We talked about the terrible predicament we find ourselves in because of their disobedience to God. And after discussing the promise and plan God had for His creation, we took the time to thoroughly examine the beautiful blessings and gifts He has for us. We discovered our new life as New Covenant believers and how we can walk in our new spiritual nature. We talked about the true Gospel of Grace and what it is not. Then I showed you some key elements to keep in mind when assessing whether something is true or not. Remember, if it isn't 100% grace, it isn't grace at all.

I hope your newfound freedom from sin and death, works and the law, and shame and self-loathing has lightened your load. I pray you have found a new joy and peace that is not regulated by your circumstances in this world. Sure, you will have hard days, but even on those days, joy and peace remain because God is with you. His grace is not only for your salvation, but it is for every moment you live between now and then. He is the victor and has shared His spoils with you.

Freedom is one of those spoils. You are free from legalism and false doctrines that keep you going in circles as you work on your sin. Jesus died for that. He already took care of your sin. He gave you a new nature that He made holy and righteous.

Now, you can embrace a freedom you never had before. Where the law and the CODE limited what you could do, you are now unlimited in what you can do for others. You are free to love, give grace freely, and release yourself from the bondage and anger of unforgiveness.

You are free to enter the throne room of God and speak to Him directly. You can go to Him. He wants to hear from you. You don't need to think for a minute that your unrighteousness keeps you from Him. In fact, He asks you to come to Him and share your life with Him.

God's radical grace has freed me from so much. Sure, I still fight with my flesh, and some days are better than others, but I have joy and peace now. I know I have value to God and a few others on this planet. I am so thankful for His grace that has healed my marriage and given me a blessed relationship with my children. I have hope for my future even though life on this planet is riddled with hardships and struggles. Life is good because God is good. I can be the Laurel God made me to be.

You can have this story too, with your own victories, your own freedom, and your own renewal. God's radical grace can heal you; I'm living proof! He asks only that you ask Him, seek Him, and believe that He offers you His revolutionary and radical grace.

We talked quite a bit about the new you. I discussed that you have a new nature in Christ. Understanding your new nature helps you to recognize why, while having been made into a new creation, you still do things that are unrighteous. You have a two-part nature now. Your old man or woman will be with you until Jesus grabs you up into His arms, but in the meantime, you have that shiny new you version that you get to walk in, because that is the *real* you.

That new *you* has been given everything you need to walk in the Spirit. You have the Spirit Himself, living in you and available for all kinds of help. His hotline is open 24/7. He can guide you when you are off track or need direction. He will offer up His fruit for you to hand out to the world around you. He intercedes for you and prays for you when you don't know what else to do or say. He will never leave you stranded.

Loving others and being present in their moments can

change lives. Draw on the wonderful characteristics that the Spirit produces in you and fully immerse yourself in them. Plant His fruit in the world around you and watch what grows.

Jesus has made you holy! You have been set apart from the world and its kingdom and have been adopted into God's kingdom and are sanctified. Just because you are holy doesn't mean you will stop sinning, but it does mean you no longer need to strive to fulfill the Jewish law or the CODE. Neither of those approaches provide an attainable goal. Because you have been born again into a new nature, you can lay down your shame at Jesus' feet. Jesus made *all things* new when He came to fix our predicament. And did He ever!

In the Book of Matthew, Jesus said that He will fill us up if we hunger and thirst for righteousness. He not only fills us up, but we become so full that we overflow. He said if we believe in Him, rivers of living water will flow from our hearts.

As we pour ourselves out, moment by moment for others, we are sharing that living water with the world around us. We simply need to be who we are in Christ: the victorious child of God.

Now that you have put your faith in Jesus' righteousness for your own, and He has remodeled you, the one thing He asks of you is to love. Love one another. Love your neighbor. Love your enemy. And love yourself, not in a selfish way, but in a caring way. If God loves you so much that He performed miracles in your life, you can love you too. You have intrinsic value, and you have a purpose while you still draw breath.

Peace and joy are available to you like you have never experienced before. Nothing stands in your way as you lean into your relationship with Jesus and see what miracles He will do if you ask Him.

So, what is next for you? Because of God's radical grace, your possibilities are limitless. Without the constraints of your old sinful nature, and because of the grace and mercy of God, you have no bounds. What desires has God placed on your heart? Where will you go, and what will you do? Whom will you love, and what will that look like?

Whatever you do and wherever God takes you, go in confidence and total faith that He is with you on your journey every step of the way. You *can* live free and unashamed now that you have embraced God's radical grace.

Appendix – Scripture References by Chapter

This Appendix does not claim to be exhaustive. It provides scripture references that support the doctrines or topics that are referred to within each chapter but may not represent all Biblical scriptures that support each doctrine or topic.

The references are listed with a segment of the sentence they relate to and are in the order in which they appear in the chapter. If a doctrine or topic is mentioned more than once in the chapter, it is usually only listed for the first time it is mentioned.

I use the New King James Version of the Bible for my personal Bible reading and study, and I appreciate the history of and accuracy of the translation, so the following references from the NKJV will best match what I am saying in the text.

The Preface

… sins were paid for by Jesus	Jhn 1:29, 1 Pe 3:18
… I knew that I had eternal salvation	Heb 5:9
… the one about us being saved by grace	Eph 2:8
… I was reading through Galatians	Gal 3, 4, 5

Giants	Num 13:33, Deu 2:11
The sun standing still	Jos 10:13
A child named Maher-Shalal-Hash-Baz	Isa 8:3
A woman turned into a pillar of salt	Gen 19:26
… God gave Moses the law	Exo 24:12
… Jesus fulfilled the requirements	Mat 5:17, Col 2:14
… trying to fulfill the law perfectly is impossible	Rom 8:7, Gal 6:13
… forgive us for our inability to do so	Act 13:38, Eph 1:7, Col 1:14
… walk in righteousness	2 Co 5:21, Phl 3:9, 1 Pe 2:24
… grace versus works	Rom 4:4, 11:6
… The Bible begins with God creating the world	Gen 1:1
Adam and Eve	Gen 3
… all humans are now born into sin	Rom 5:12-19
… including you and me	Rom 3:10, 3:23
Like the great King David…	1 Sa 13:14, Acts 13:22
… with sin came death	Rom 6:23
… aware we are not righteous	Gal 3:19-25
… we cannot make ourselves righteous	Rom 3:10, 4:5-6, Gal 2:21
We cannot be with God if we are not righteous…	Mat 25:46, 1 Cor 6:9-11
… first hint of this plan	Gen 3:15
… by chapter 12	Gen 12:3

... this is the Abrahamic Covenant	Gen 17:7, 22:15-18
... the New Covenant that Jesus spoke about	Mat 26:28, Mar 14:24
This deal ... with Abraham...	Jhn 1:17
... Jesus, who is the solution	Jhn 3:16-17
... answer for our new life	Eph 4:24, 2 Cor 5:17
... Jesus' ministry	Luk 3:23
... conquer sin and death	Rom 5:12-21
... impart His righteousness	Rom 3:21-22
... we have a very different mission	Jhn 15:12
... He is the foundation	Luk 6:47-48
... and author of the Bible	Jhn 1:1, 14
... story of Cleopas and another man	Luk 24:13-32
... Jesus is the Messiah, or Savior	Act 13:23
... Jesus' death and resurrection	Luk 23:33, 24:6
... I realized we can find Him foreshadowed	Num 21:8-9 (Jhn 3:14), Exo 17:6 (1 Co 10:4)
... and prophesied about	Isa 53 (Mat 26:57-68, 27:27-50)
... Noah and the flood	Gen 7, 8
... Book of Judges	Judges
There is action...	Exodus
... adventure	Joshua
... humor	Proverbs 11:22, 1 Kings 18:26-27, Heb 11:12
... romance	Ruth

… suspense	1 Sa 24
There is quantum physics…	Act 8:39-40,
	Jhn 20:19
… and miracles	Num 22:21-35,
	Exo 7:8-10:23,
	Jdg 6:37-40,
	Jhn 11:38-44
… family stories are included	Gen 37:1-50:26,
	Esther, Ruth

Chapter 4 – The Fall

Fall of Man	Gen 3
… all people born…are born into unrighteousness	Rom 3:10
… our flesh is unrighteous because of Adam's sin	Rom 5:12-21
… hangs around until we shed it	1 Cor 15:42-50
… death came in also	Rom 5:12-21
… cannot live in eternity if we are unrighteous	1 Cor 6:9
It has to do with your faith…	Rom 3:28, 5:1-2,
	Gal 2:16, 3:11,
	Eph 2:8
… not dependent on *how much* we've sinned	Jas 2:10-11
… born new in Him	Jhn 3:3, Eph 4:24,
	1 Pet 1:23
… sins are forgiven	Act 13:38, Eph 1:7,
	Col 1:14
… we escape death	Rom 5:14-17, 6:23

If they obeyed the LORD's commands…	Exo 19:5-6
… nation of Israel didn't hold up	Jer 31:31-32
It is impossible to perfectly fulfill the law…	Heb 10:1-4
… law was given so	Rom 5:20, 7:7
… I was a sinner, and I needed a Savior	Mat 1:21, 1 Ti 1:15
… our righteousness can't come by the law.	Rom 4:13, Gal 2:21, Phl 3:8-9
… law was ineffective at making people perfect.	Heb 7:18-19, 10:1
… falls short of God's glorious righteousness.	Rom 3:23
… Christ was able to fulfill the law. He was without sin.	Matt 5:17 Heb 4:15
… He released us from it.	Gal 3:5-29
… Jesus nailed the written requirements	Col 2:14
… He told you to love Him and love others.	Jhn 14:21, 15:12, 1 Jo 3:11, 23
… There is no law against loving others.	Gal 5:22-23
… new deal is much better	Heb 8:6
… forgiveness for our sins	Act 13:38, Eph 1:7, Col 1:14
… His righteousness to us	Rom 3:21-26
… avoid eating shellfish	Lev 11:9-12
… offering a sacrifice for our sins	Lev 16:5
… God wrote His law on your heart	Jer 31:33

… not under the law, but under	Rom 6:14

Chapter 7 – The New Covenant

… Mediator of the New Covenant	Heb 9:15
… New Covenant is a better covenant	Heb 7:20-22, 8:4-6
… ministry a "more excellent ministry."	Heb 8:6
… Mosaic Covenant	Exo 19:5-6
… Jewish nation couldn't fulfill	Jer 31:31-32
… always been about faith in Jesus	Rom 3:30
… from Eden to Mt. Moriah to Golgotha	Gen 3:15, Gen 22:1-18, Mat 27:33-54
… Israelites had to continuously	Heb 10:1-4
… the law reveals to us that we are sinners	Gal 3:24-25
… sin abounded, grace abounded much more	Rom 5:20
… sacrificial death was the beginning	Mar 14:24, Heb 9:15
… free gift of eternal life	Jhn 10:28, Rom 6:23
… it is also about a new life now	Rom 6:4, Eph 2:4-5. 2 Co 3:6
… through the prophet Jeremiah	Jer 31:33-34
… sin was in the world.	Rom 5:13
… Abraham's faith as righteousness	Gen 15:6
… obedience to the law	Exo 19:5-6

… all about faith.	Rom 3:28, 5:1-2, Gal 2:16, 3:11, Eph 2:8
… we are imputed the very righteousness of Christ.	Rom 4:20-25
… prophets investigated the message of grace	1 Pet 1:10-12
… parable of the wine skins.	Mat 9:17, Mar 2:22, Luk 5:37-39
… Jesus called His cup of wine	Mat 26:28, Mar 14:24, Luk 22:20
… no one desires new wine	Luk 5:39

Chapter 8 – The CODE

… Ten Commandments	Exo 20:1-17
… Feasts of God	Lev 23
… and not getting a tattoo were ignored	Lev 19:28
… in Hebrews chapter ten	Heb 10:24-25
I avoided drinking wine and eating pork.	Eph 5:18, Lev 11:4-7
… God made us righteous	Rom 3:21-22
… and gave us what we need to love	Eze 36:26, Rom 5:5, Gal 5:22, 2 Ti 1:7
… scripture in 2 Timothy that helps	2 Ti 3:16-17
He already made us holy…	Acts 26:15-18, 1 Co 6:11, Heb 10:10
After calling the Galatians foolish …	Gal 3:1

… become perfect by doing things in their flesh.	Gal 3:3
… into His spiritual kingdom.	Col 1:13, 2:20-23
… in his letter to the Romans.	Rom 7:6
… in his letter to the Corinthians.	2 Co 3:5-6
… love God and love others	Jhn 13:34, 14:15, 15:12
… God decided to die for us	Heb 2:9
… give us a new heart	Eze 36:26
… sent His Spirit	Jhn 14:26, Gal 4:6

Chapter 9 – The Love of God

… loves me so much	Eph 2:4-7
Jesus wants everyone to be saved.	Mat 18:14, 1 Ti 2:3-4, 2 Pe 3:9
True love serves others.	Gal 5:13
… people are sinful and unrighteous	Rom 3:10, 5:8
… He went to the cross	Mat 27:35, Mar 15:24, Luk 23:33, Jhn 19:17-18
His purpose in coming was to serve …	Mat 20:28
… to enjoy fellowship with Him.	Jhn 14:2-3, Rev 21:3-4
… God is love	1 Jo 4:8
… true love does not condemn.	Jhn 3:17, 8:10-11, Rom 8:1
… legalistic Pharisees.	Mat 15:1-14

… believing their righteousness was good	Mat 23:13
You are His poem, His masterpiece…	Eph 2:10

Chapter 10 – The Separation Lie

Unbelievers *are* separated from God…	Eph 2:13, 1 Cor 6:9-10
The concept that sin separates us…	Isa 59
They couldn't go past the veil…	Heb 9:1-8
… past the veil, and into His presence	Heb 9:11-26
… we had no hope and were without God.	Eph 2:11-12
… we have been brought near to God	Eph 2:13
… nothing can separate us from God's love.	Rom 8:38-39
… Spirit dwells in those who have faith	1 Co 3:16, 1 Th 4:8, 2 Tim 1:14
… He justifies us freely	Rom 3:21-26

Chapter 11 – The Duality

… Fruit of the Spirit	Gal 5:22-23
… Ten Commandments	Exo 20:1-17
… we are a new creation in Christ	2 Co 5:17
… we have been born *again*.	Jhn 3:3
… into our sinful nature	Rom 3:10
… a second time by the Spirit	Jhn 3:5-6
… into our new godly nature.	2 Pet 1:3-4

… have a two-part nature	Rom 8:3-11
… until I leave it behind	1 Co 15:42, 44, 46, 50-53, Phl 3:21
… not as a man-pleaser	Eph 6:5-7
… esteems others higher than myself	Phl 2:3
… our real citizenship	Jhn 17:14, Eph 2:19, Phl 3:20
… our sinful nature of flesh the *old man*.	Rom 6:6, Col 3:9
… it grows corrupt.	Eph 4:22
… it profits us nothing	Jhn 6:63
… we should have no confidence in it!	Phl 3:3
… flesh is weak	Mar 14:38
… doesn't make our flesh able to obey	Col 2:20-23
… flesh is what drives us into temptation.	Jas 1:14
… stop giving our flesh control	Rom 6:12
… power that the Spirit gives us	Gal 5:22-23
Paul calls it our *new man*.	Eph 4:24, Col 3:10
Our spirit is revived.	Eze 36:26, 2 Cor 5:17
… are baptized by the Holy Spirit.	Mar 1:8, 1 Co 12:13
… verse in 2 Corinthians	2 Cor 5:17
… Ezekiel gives us insight	Eze 36:26-27
… imputed the very righteousness	Rom 4:20-25
… It is made holy	Acts 26:18, 1 Co 1:2, 6:11

… totally separate from our old self.	Gal 5:17
… Spirit guides	Jhn 16:13
… comforts	Acts 9:31
… and helps	Jhn 14:26
… no longer slaves of sin	Rom 6:6
… God will give us a way to escape.	2 Co 10:13
In chapter seven …	Rom 7
… was crucified with Jesus	Gal 5:24
Rest like God said you could.	Mat 11:28-29

Chapter 12 – The Blessings

… even if you break only one of the laws	Jas 2:10
… we are all born into sin.	Rom 3:10
God wrote that into your heart.	Jer 31:33
… walk in Him	Gal 5:25
That higher calling is to love.	Jhn 13:34, 1 Jo 3:23, 4:21
… sin is the farthest from our minds.	Gal 5:16
… He made us righteous and holy	Rom 3:21-22, 4:5-6, 5:17, Acts 26:18, 1 Co 1:2, 6:11
… gave us His Spirit	1 Co 3:16, 1 Th 4:8, 2 Tim 1:14
… covenant with Abraham promised	Gen 22:15-18
… every spiritual blessing.	Eph 1:3
… justification refers to	Rom 3:26, 4:25, 5:16-18

... He imputes His righteousness	Rom 4:6, 11
... by being obedient or trying to obey the law	Act 13:39, Rom 3:20, 28, Gal 2:16, 3:11
... unrighteous and that we need a Savior	Gal 3:22-25
... verse in Second Timothy	2 Ti 3:16-17
... is delivered into His spiritual kingdom.	Col 1:13
... after washing his feet	Jhn 13:1-10
... they were washed, sanctified, and justified	1 Co 6:11
... no longer a slave to his sin	Rom 6:6
... but to righteousness.	Rom 6:18-19
... even our enemies	Mat 5:4
... prophet Ezekiel told us	Eze 36:26-27
... love our neighbors	Luk 10:27, Rom 13:9-10, Gal 5:14, Jas 2:8

Chapter 13 – The Sanctification Myth

... contrary to *already being* holy	Act 20:32, 26:18, 1 Co 1:2, 6:11, 7:14, Heb 10:10, Jde 1:1
... our flesh only grows more corrupt	Eph 4:22
... not be discouraged in suffering	2 Co 1:3-5
... minds are blinded, and their hearts are veiled	2 Co 3:14-15
... blindness is lifted in Christ	2 Co 3:16

Although we are hard-pressed…	2 Co 4:8-9
… just spent the previous eleven verses	2 Co 3:7-17
… law can only condemn us	Rom 4:15
Working on sin is the opposite of grace.	Rom 11:6
… sin doesn't have control	Rom 6:6-7
Jesus already forgave…	Act 13:38, Eph 1:7, Col 1:14
… not under the law	Rom 6:14, Gal 3:13-14, 18
… we can rest in Him.	Mat 11:28-29

Chapter 14 – The Walk

… we live in the Spirit, we should walk in Him.	Gal 5:25
… love others as God has loved us	Eph 5:2
… letter to the Ephesians	Eph 4:22-24
He is the Spirit of God.	Rom 8:9, 1 Co 3:16
… one member of the triune God	Jhn 4:24, 10:10, Mat 28:19, 1 Jo 5:7
… convict the world of sin	Jhn 16:7-8
… testify about Jesus	Jhn 15:26
… guarantee of our salvation	2 Co 1:22, 5:5, Eph 1:13-14
… baptized with Him	Mar 1:8
The Spirit sanctifies and justifies…	1 Co 6:11
… send the Helper	Jhn 14:26, 15:26, 16:7
… intercede for us	Rom 8:26

He is our guide…	Jhn 16:13
He gives us spiritual gifts…	1 Co 12:4-11
… produces godly fruit in us	Gal 5:22-23, Eph 5:8-9
He comforts…	Acts 9:31
… and leads us as we walk in Him	Rom 8:14, Gal 5:18
… as mercy, not sacrifice	Mat 9:13, 12:7
… it is impossible for us to be in our flesh.	Gal 5:16
… in the Book of Philippians.	Phl 1:15-18
He called them hypocrites…	Mat 23:1-33
… they were like whitewashed tombs	Mat 23:27

Chapter 15 – The Light Switch

… switching to the Light	Mat 5:14-16, Jhn 8:12, 9:5
… esteem others higher than ourselves	Phil 2:3
We put on love.	Col 3:14
He said in Ephesians…	Eph 4:22-24
… we no longer live in darkness	Jhn 8:12, Luk 11:35-36
… is greater than he who is in the world.	1 Jo 4:4
When we are born of the Spirit…	Jhn 3:8
… God will work all things out for his good	Rom 8:28
… walking by faith, not sight.	2 Co 5:7

… our Light switch	Mat 5:14, Eph 5:8, 1 Th 5:5, 1 Pe 2:9

Chapter 16 – The Law of Love

God is the force of all creation…	Gen 1:1
… He is love.	1 Jo 4:8
… the new law of God	Jhn 13:34, 15:12, Rom 13:9
… under the law of Moses	Rom 6:14
… freed from the bondage of sin and death	Rom 8:2
… He was giving them a new commandment	Jhn 13:34
… this new commandment	1 Jo 2:7-8
… we have been made righteous	Rom 3:21-22, 4:5-6, 5:17, Acts 26:18, 1 Co 1:2, 6:11
… given a new spirit	Eze 36:26, Eph 4:23
… along with the Holy Spirit	1 Co 3:16, 1 Th 4:8, 2 Tim 1:14
… demonstrating His love for us	Rom 5:8
… the devil's mission	Jhn 10:10
… when God touches lives, life happens.	Rom 8:6-11
… love our enemies.	Mat 5:44
… I could see past their flaws	2 Co 5:16
… fruits of the Holy Spirit	Gal 5:22-23
… Love does no harm	Rom 13:10

Chapter 17 – The Freedom

… the Ten Commandments	Exo 20:1-17
… "love your neighbor" is all about?	Mat 22:39, Rom 13:9, Gal 5:14
… possible for us to be free.	Jhn 8:32, 36, Rom 8:2, Gal 5:1
We are free from sin.	Rom 6:18-22, 8:2
… sin put on our account. We are forgiven.	Rom 4:5-8, Col 2:13-14
… walk in the Spirit	Rom 8:4, Gal 5:16, 25
… freed from our old sinful nature	Rom 6
… His child	Jhn 1:12, Rom 8:16
… a royal priesthood	1 Pet 2:9
… friend of Jesus	Jhn 15:13, 15
… a citizen of the heavenly kingdom.	Jhn 17:16, 18:36, Eph 2:19
… His workmanship	Eph 2:10
… a new creation	2 Cor 5:17
… more than a conqueror.	Rom 8:37
… salt of the earth	Mat 5:13
… light of the world.	Mat 5:14, Eph 5:8
… loving, supporting, and serving one another	Gal 5:13, 6:2
… not to use our freedom to cover	1 Pe 2:16
… no longer under the Jewish law.	Rom 6:14
… fulfill His new law of love.	Mat 22:37-39, Jhn 13:34
… everything we do should be in love.	1 Co 16:14

… perfect love casts out our fear.	1 Jo 4:18
… He loved us first.	1 Jo 4:19
… God does chasten	Heb 12:6
… His punishment	Mat 25:46, 2 Th 1:3-9, Heb 10:28-29
… I am Your child	Jhn 1:12, Rom 8:16
… Jesus has redeemed	Rom 3:24, 1 Co 1:30, Eph 1:7
… I can come boldly to Your throne	Heb 4:16
… that brings repentance	Rom 2:4
Our mission…	Mar 16:15
When they ask you…	1 Pe 3:15

Chapter 21 – The Boot Strap Gospel

… everyday life based on works	Rom 11:6
… a false gospel.	2 Co 11:4, Gal 1:6-7, 2:4-5
… be a new creation	2 Co 5:17
… already sanctified	Act 20:32, 26:18, 1 Co 1:2 6:11, Heb 10:10
… and died for them	Rom 5:8
… we shed it on our way to eternity.	1 Co 15:50-53
… striving and working so you could love!	Gal 3:10-11, Eph 5:2
… a New Covenant believer	Mat 26:28, Heb 9:15
… a future citizen of the spiritual kingdom	Jhn 17:14, Jas 2:5

… freed from the law	Rom 8:2
… walking in the Spirit	Rom 8:1,4, Gal 5:16, 25
… we are all sinners	Rom 3:23
… serve in the newness of the Spirit.	Rom 7:6
… he got back up and pressed on.	Phl 3:12-14
… daily rest in Jesus.	Mat 11:28, Heb 4:10

Chapter 22 – The Keys

… no one should take what is preached	Acts 17:11
… no one stands between you and God.	Jer 31:33-34
… Spirit makes some of us teachers.	1 Co 12:28, Eph 4:11
… Jesus ushered in the New Covenant	Mat 26:28, Heb 9:15
… which created an "I will" relationship	Jer 31:31-33
While we were sinners…	Rom 5:8
… fellow citizens to obey	Exo 19:5, Jer 7:23, 11:4
… go through the priests	Exo 40:15, Lev 16:30-34, Heb 9:6-7
… new High Priest	Heb 2:27, 3:1, 4:14, 7:26
… Mediator of this new deal.	1 Ti 2:5, Heb 12:24
… between you and the Father.	Jhn 14:6

… boldly to His throne	Heb 4:16
John, Luke, and Paul…	Jhn 1:17, Acts 13:38-39, Rom 6:14
… make sin abound	Rom 5:20
… reveal the world needed a Savior.	Gal 3:22-25
Jesus already fulfilled the law…	Mat 5:17
… freeing you from the bondage	Rom 8:2
… old man and putting on the new	Eph 4:22-24
… walking in the newness of life.	Rom 6:4
… born of water and the Spirit.	Jhn 3:5
… Paul narrates his struggle	Rom 7
… a new creation in Christ	2 Co 5:17
… still have temptations.	1 Co 10:13, Gal 6:1, Heb 2:18
… spirit is at odds with your flesh.	Gal 5:17
… justified	Rom 1:17, 3:21-22, 4:5-6, 5:18-19, 6:18, 9:30, 10:4, 10
… been sanctified	Act 20:32, 26:18, 1 Co 1:2, 6:11, 7:14, Heb 10:10
Walking in righteousness…	2 Ti 3:16, 1 Jo 3:10
… in the Spirit	Rom 8:4, Gal 5:16, 25
He helps you…	Jhn 14:26, 15:26, Rom 8:26
… guides you	Jhn 16:13
… produces fruit in you	Gal 5:22-23, Eph 5:9

… intercedes for you	Rom 8:26
… Bible is all about Jesus.	Luk 24:27
Then it's not the Gospel.	Mar 1:1
… Jesus imputing His righteousness	Rom 4:5-8, 10:4
… power of the Spirit to work	Act 1:8, Rom 15:13, 2 Ti 1:7
… it is about works, not grace	Rom 11:6
… to participate in your sanctification?	Heb 10:10
Jesus specifically warned us…	Mat 16:12, Luk 12:1
… by man's traditions and teachings.	Col 2:8, 18-23

Chapter 23 – The Throne

… I talked about Adam and Eve	Gen 3
… naked… cover themselves	Gen 3:7
… try to hide from God.	Gen 3:8
… He asked	Gen 3:9
He not only covered them…	Gen 3:21
… He also had a plan	Jer 31:31-34
… God is for us, not against us.	Rom 8:31
… Adam and Eve created a separation	Rom 5:18, Eph 2:12
Jesus was sent …	Eph 2:13
… we have a whole new gig.	Heb 8:1-6
… tabernacle of God.	Exo 25:8-9
… Most Holy Place	Exo 26:33
God spoke from above the mercy seat…	Exo 25:22

… or priests, could not enter	Lev 16:2
… extensive ceremonial consecration.	Exo 29
… Jesus is the High Priest	Heb 2:17, 3:1, 4:14, 9:11
… veil in the temple was torn	Mat 27:51, Mar 15:38, Luk 23:45
That event was symbolic…	Heb 10:19-22
… heavenly veil of Jesus' flesh	Heb 10:20
We can go with the full assurance…	Heb 10:22
… because we *have* been washed	1 Co 6:11
… made righteous.	Rom 3:21-22, 4:5-6, 5:18-19, 9:30, 10:4, 10
… that helps us when we need it.	Heb 4:16
… seek His strength	2 Co 12:9
… to escape temptation.	1 Co 10:13

Chapter 24 – The Moment

… He has made us righteous	Rom 3:21-22, 4:5-6, 5:18-19, 9:30, 10:4, 10
… we are His children	Jhn 1:12, Rom 8:16, 1 Jo 3:2
… Jesus' grace is sufficient	2 Co 12:9
… He would be with us and never leave us.	Deu 31:8, Heb 13:5-6
… God knows the number of our days	Job 14:5

… already made holy	Act 20:32, 26:18, 1 Co 1:2, 6:11, 7:14, Heb 10:10, Jde 1:1
… righteousness that Jesus has imputed	Rom 1:17, 3:21-22, 4:5-6, 5:18-19, 6:18, 9:30, 10:4, 10
… offers His divine power	Act 1:8, Rom 15:13, 2 Ti 1:7
… law out of our way	Col 2:14
… no longer our master.	Gal 3:24-25
Love is the only thing…	Jhn 13:34
… verse in Psalms	Psa 118:24
God tells us in Jeremiah…	Jer 29:11
… all things together for good	Rom 8:28
Jesus told us His yoke is easy…	Matt 11:30
… rejoice when we are going through	Jhn 16:33, Phl 4:4
… we can grab His hand	Psa 63:7-8
Like Paul says in Philippians…	Phl 3:12
… God will tell us we did good	Mat 25:21

Chapter 25 – The Victory

… bring salvation to the world.	Jhn 3:17
… defeated sin's control and death	Rom 6:6, 1 Co 15:26, 54, 57
He has overcome the enemy…	Heb 2:14
He has brought us out of darkness…	1 Pe 2:9
… encouraged in the Book of John	Jhn 16:33
… greater than the enemy	1 Jo 4:4

… we need not despair	2 Co 4:8
… our strength and our refuge.	Psa 28:8, 46:1
There is nothing we can't do in Him.	Phl 4:13
… life that demonstrates freedom	Jhn 8:36
… we are holy and righteous	1 Co 6:11, Heb 10:10, Rom 3:21-22, 4:5-6, 10:10
… freed from the control of sin.	Rom 6:6
… Creator of the universe	Gen 1
… Our joy is full	Jhn 15:11, 16:24
… underlying peace	Phl 4:6-7
… Jesus washed the disciples' feet Jhn	13:12

Chapter 26 – The End, Or Is It the Beginning?

… Adam and Eve.	Gen 3
… the promise and plan	Gen 15:4, 17:21, 22:15-18
… discovered our new life	2 Cor 5:17, 2 Pet 1:3-4
… walk in our new spiritual nature.	Gal 5:25
… Gospel of Grace	Rom 3:23, 6:23, 5:8, 10:9, 10:10, 10:4, 6:14, 13:14, 7:6, 13:10, 8:4, 8:5
… if it isn't 100% grace	Rom 11:6
… freedom from sin and death	Rom 5:14-17, Eph 1:7, Col 1:14

… works and the law	Mat 5:17, Rom 11:6, Col 2:14
… a new joy and peace	Jhn 15:11, 16:24, Phl 4:6-7
He is the victor …	1 Co 15:57
Jesus died for that.	Act 13:38, Eph 1:7, Col 1:14
… new nature	Jhn 3:3, 6, 2 Co 5:17
… made holy and righteous.	Act 26:18, Rom 5:19, 10:4, 10, 1 Co 1:2, 6:11, Heb 10:10
… enter the throne room of God	Heb 10:19-20
… you have a new nature	2 Co 5:17, Eph 4:24, Col 3:10
… old man or woman will be with you	1 Co 15:52-53
… need to walk in the Spirit.	Gal 5:16, 25
You have the Spirit…	Rom 8:9-11, 1 Co 3:16
He can guide…	Jhn 16:13
… offer up His fruit	Gal 5:22-23
He intercedes for you and prays…	Rom 8:26-27
… made *all things* new	2 Co 5:17
… hunger and thirst for righteousness.	Mat 5:6
… rivers of living water	Jhn 7:38
Love one another.	Jhn 13:34
Love your neighbor.	Mar 12:31
Love your enemy.	Mat 5:44

Notes

[1] Simone, F. (2017). *Negative Self-Talk: Don't Let It Overwhelm You.* Psychology Today. www.psychologytoday.com/us/blog/family-affair/201712/negative-self-talk-dont-let-it-overwhelm-you

[2] Serious Facts. (n.d.). *40 Interesting Bible Facts.* www.seriousfacts.com/bible-facts

[3] Smietana, B. (2017). *Lifeway Research: Americans Are Fond of the Bible, Don't Actually Read It.* Lifeway Research. lifewayresearch.com/2017/04/25/lifeway-research-americans-are-fond-of-the-bible-dont-actually-read-it

[4] Copyright © 2006 Rising Springs Music (ASCAP) worshiptogether.com Songs (ASCAP) Vamos Publishing (ASCAP) (adm. at CapitolCMGPublishing.com) All rights reserved. Used by permission.

[5] Smietana, B. (2017). *Most Americans Admit They're Sinners.* Lifeway Research. lifewayresearch.com/2017/08/15/most-americans-admit-theyre-sinners

[6] Brown, R.M. (1983). *Sudden Death: A Novel.* Bantam Books.

[7] Boynton, C. W. (2014). *Connecticut Witch Trials: The First Panic in the New World.* The History Press.

Author's Note

I would like to thank you for reading my book. I pray you have discovered God's beautiful and unfailing grace for yourself as you walk a little lighter and with more joy. I would love it if you would connect with me. Following are ways in which you can do just that.

You can receive my quarterly newsletter, insider perks, updates on blogs, and news about what I am up to by visiting:
www.laurelappel.com/emailsignup

Or simply scan this code:

By subscribing to my email list, you will also receive a special invitation to join the discussion about *Radical Grace: Live Free and Unashamed* in my Book Club group on Facebook. You can find me on Facebook here. I'd love to hear from you:
facebook.com/LaurelAppelAuthor

You may also follow me on Instagram here:
instagram.com/laurelappel

Or Twitter here:
twitter.com/AppelLaurel

You may also let me know what you think by leaving an honest review anywhere my book is sold or on Good-reads.

Again, thank you for reading, and I hope to hear from you soon!

Laurel

About the Author

 **LAUREL APPEL** is an author, freelance writer, speaker, and podcast host. She has over twenty-five years of experience studying and teaching the Bible and has written Bible studies for both adults and children. She is a survivor of childhood sexual abuse and has overcome agoraphobia, OCD, and self-harm through her extensive pursuit of God's grace. She lives and ministers with her husband, Phil, in North Carolina. For more info, visit LaurelAppel.com.

CPSIA information can be obtained
at www.ICGtesting.com
Printed in the USA
BVHW071423261222
654959BV00018B/626/J